Reiki Plus®

Professional Practitioner's Manual

for

Second Degree

A Guide for Spiritual Healing

by

Richelle M. Jarrell, Reiki Master

and

David G. Jarrell, Reiki Master

707 Barcelona Rd.
Key Largo, Florida 33037
(305) 451-9881 Fax (305) 451-9841
WWW.Reikiplus.com Email: Reikiplus@mindspring.com

First Edition, July 8, 1992
Second Edition, April 14, 1995
Third Edition, August 1, 2000

Privacy Act for Protection of Sacred Knowledge

In respect for the sacred knowledge entrusted to you when initiated to Second Degree, you are asked not to verbalize the words of the symbols or share the mystical symbols with the uninitiated. To do so diffuses the energy due to the lack of respect for sacred knowledge.

Copyright and Legal Notice of Registered Marks

Foreign Language Publications

These titles are available in both Spanish and Portuguese: *Reiki Plus Natural Healing* and the *Reiki Plus Professional Practitioner's Manual for Second Degree.*

Service Marks

Notice of Registration: the service mark **Reiki-Plus®** was issued to Reverend David G. Jarrell. After completion of the *Reiki Plus* Practitioner Certification Program a student is authorized to advertise himself as a Practitioner of *Reiki Plus* and to use the Registered Mark of **Reiki Plus®** on business cards and brochures.

We Dedicate this Third Edition

To the Teachers of *Reiki Plus*, past, present and future, who have spent many years to provide to the student of natural healing an opportunity to reach his or her dreams and to become a highly trained *Reiki Plus* Practitioner.

Art

Front Cover: David G. Jarrell
Diagram: Rosie Voreadou
Photograph: Bob Care

A Warm Thank You for Editing Assistance

Otono Johnston, Shirley Boring and Betty Everett

Table of Contents

Introduction to the Third Edition

Reiki Plus Professional Practitioner's Manual for Second Degree was first published in July 1992, and made professional Practitioner's training for Second Degree available to all students of Reiki. In 1995 the revised Second Edition was printed. The Second Edition has been translated by Spanish and Portuguese publishers, along with David's first title, *Reiki Plus Natural Healing*.

In this Third Edition you will find a complete reworking of the previous Editions. Not only in a new book size format, the book has been expanded to embrace the additional years of experience gained from teaching and private practice since the First Edition in 1992. The First and Second Edition had six chapters. The Second Edition added the *Forgiveness Meditation* and a new cover design. The Third Edition has expanded to eleven exciting and information-filled chapters.

You will find this almost a completely new book. Chapters Three and Four teach treatment and client relations. Chapter Six presents the *Psycho-Therapeutic Reiki Plus* concept and its relationship to the Laws of Transmutation. Chapter Seven is devoted to a new forgiveness technique for healing the Inner Child and the adult self. Chapter Eight presents the *Twenty-One Day Healing Cycle* and how it relates to the Healing Curve and the emotional layering of somatic memory. Chapter Nine expands the "I-Thy-Divine" concept of healing and spiritual evolution.

The last chapter of all editions has presented how to treat specific imbalances most commonly found in the healing room of the natural healer. In this Third Edition we have added additional specific imbalances and updated the entire listing with additional nutritional material. Richelle has included specific herbal combinations that are historically known to support the body systems involved. This chapter presents reference material useful to all Reiki Practitioners, from First Degree to Master.

The Journey of the Authors into Healing

The evolution of this book dates back to David's earliest awareness and later his first paranormal and spiritual experiences. From age six until eleven he allowed his parents to dictate his participation in the religion of their choice. In the beginning he found comfort in staring at the auric field painted in gold around the head of Jesus. At age ten, in the fall of 1956 as Uranus conjuncted his Mercury, David began spontaneous astral traveling. During this time he heard a voice in his mind's ear that he would one-day visit Japan, England and Greece.

Near the time of Easter 1957, his dad accidentally ran over one of his kittens, which he buried. David had spent the day and evening away with a friend. When he asked his dad if he put a cross over the grave, he was told, "no." He asked his dad why not? And he answered, "because a cat does not have a soul." This is when he knew that he no longer belonged spiritually or philosophically with his genetic family. He knew, but yet did not yet have the words or understanding, to explain his relationship to the subtle planes and the ascended masters. This would come a few years later. So, as Saturn trined his ascendant, his spiritual search began in a town void of spiritual teachers—fortunately David knew to keep his paranormal experiences quiet, until he met like-minded friends.

At the age of fourteen he further developed and honed his senses by starting his lifelong love of scuba diving. Spending countless hours in the murky coastline waters of North Carolina sensitized his etheric body field to feel the unseen. During the summer of his fourteenth year he was obsessed with the fighter pilots of WWI. Having read every book available in his hometown library, he knew that he had lived in this time period. Later during his first visit to England in 1981, he would find his connection to his Irish past life and the date of his youthful death.

College followed high school, as did the Vietnam conflict and his eventual inward search for self-healing in 1967, at the significant age of twenty-one, while stationed in Korea as a member of the United States Army Security Agency. From January 1968 until March 1970, David spent the remainder of his military duty in the country of Japan. During these two years he became vegetarian, practiced yoga and meditation, was head scuba instructor on the base and also carried out his top-secret military duties.

Upon his discharge from military service in March 1970, David was exposed to the teachings of the ascended masters, and spiritual and medical astrology. What followed in the fall of 1971 would eventually direct his destiny in the field of natural healing. He was taught by his spiritual teachers how to develop his natural healing ability to release and extract pain and discord from the physical body to a safer and higher form of healing: Etheric Body balancing and the use of the Violet Ray of healing. This healing modality was to become known as ***PSEB***, Physio-Spiritual Etheric Body healing in the summer of 1982. For the next several years David further developed his understanding of healing and the mystical world of spirit, providing professional astrological and clairvoyant readings. Communicating with the spirit world became second nature, as did hearing their messages. During this time David was professionally practicing astrology in Raleigh, N.C.

The New Year of 1975 David left the full-time exploration of the mystical world and private practice to venture into his next and important phase of training, the corporate world of business. He entered knowing that he would, at the right time, hear the call to return full time to the world he left behind. During the years in the field of shopping center management and development, he used his gifts quietly in the daily discharge of his corporate responsibilities. This was the time his spiritual teachers knew that he needed training in business management.

In the spring of 1979 David began to transition from the corporate life back into the private practice of astrology and healing. During the summer of 1980 he heard about Reiki healing and a teacher named Virginia Samdhal. Virginia was the first student of Takata to be trained and initiated as a Reiki Master. He was told by his spiritual teachers that his next step was to pursue the study of Reiki, and so he did. Sight unseen, he arranged with Virginia to sponsor her to the Durham-Chapel Hill area of North Carolina to teach Reiki First Degree in October of 1980. Then in the January snowstorm of 1981 her return visit yielded his Second Degree training and initiation. In the spring David became the first student of Virginia's to prepare with her for Mastership. David never had the opportunity to meet Mrs. Takata.

Mrs. Takata having passed over on December 11, 1980, paved the new and unproven testing ground of her twenty-one personally trained teachers to now become teachers of teachers. (The twenty-second teacher was actually initiated by her own husband, and was later accepted by Takata as a Reiki Master.)

Following his January initiation into Second Degree, his spiritual teachers directed David that he should spend the new moon in Aquarius in the mountains of North Carolina, as an important event would occur at this time. The guidance was followed, and the event marked his spiritual initiation to fully awaken his kundalini. This initiation was observed by a close friend who drew a picture of the Tibetan spiritual teacher in spirit who performed David's initiation. David was told that each time his teacher touched his Crown Chakra, he went into an altered state and his body would awaken thrashing forwards and backwards like a serpent. David remembered the touch of the teacher's hand on his head and the serpent movement of energy up his spine, which he felt lasted for only a few minutes. This experience occurred three times during this meditation period. What David did not learn until the summer of 1998 from this same friend, was that this brief event lasted not a few minutes, but transpired over a continuous period of several hours. As David looks back upon this experience today, he can truly say that the statement that "there is no time and space in the spiritual dimension" is the only way to explain how several hours were experienced as a continuous kundalini release stimulated by three contacts to his head. The inception of *Reiki Plus* occurred this 5th day of February 1981 on the new moon in Aquarius.

In the following six months David trained with Virginia Samdahl, co-teaching Reiki classes in different cities on the east coast. Virginia asked David to firmly commit to teaching Reiki in the time honored manner that Mrs. Takata had taught Virginia. He searched his heart and knew that although he loved and respected Virginia and her teachings, he could not make a life long commitment to only teach in her manner.

So, following his heart he asked that he be guided to another Reiki Teacher. In August, he traveled to Chicago and finished his training with Barbara McCullough on August 5th 1981. Interestingly this date followed six months by the calendar date from the date of his Initiation from the Ascended Master, referred to as Mr. T. by David, that fated February day.

In the month of November of 1981 David was invited by Phyllis Furumoto to visit her in Nelson, B.C. Canada. Phyllis is the granddaughter of Takata, and had been trained to Mastership by her. So, David spent a week in Nelson, meeting several other Reiki Masters that Takata had trained and getting to know Phyllis and her former husband Michael and his kids. In March of the following year, Phyllis joined David in Sarasota Florida where he was teaching a Reiki One Class. They spent the weekend co-teaching this class and sharing with each other their perspectives on the spiritual Art of Reiki.

David's journey to the distant lands predicted at an early age have all been visited, and still are today. David had the pleasure to be the first presenter on the subject of Reiki in England's Festival of Mind-Body and Spirit in London in July of 1982. He followed his lecture a few days later with his first Reiki Class in England. A student from Greece attended this workshop and invited him to Greece the following year to teach in Athens. David and Richelle still teach in Greece thanks to the initial efforts of this student, who is also the artist that drew the artwork for this book and *Reiki Plus Natural Healing*. Today, David and Richelle travel and teach in Solaniki, where one of the *Reiki Plus Masters* resides with her family. Visiting Greece is in so many ways to David going home, especially when he has the time to visit Crete.

There are so many feelings and experiences that could be shared about David's life as a teacher of Reiki since 1981, and as a practitioner in the mystical arts since 1971, that a resting point must be considered. It does prepare the thoughts for a book pertaining to the professional life he has led, and maybe one day will be inspired to share with his readers and students.

What is important to end these words about his life for you the reader of this Third Edition, is that each person chooses to be born at the right time, in the right place and to the right parents, that each of us might unfold the plan we made before incarnating this time around. Everyone is a special soul and as David always says to his clients in challenging crisis and students in growth situations: you, no one else, is the most important person in the unfolding and healing of your ego participating in your soul's journey. So, you, yes you reading these words, are invited to remember that each soul is equally important in the grand scheme of God's Divine Plan. If each of us will lift up our consciousness and stare fate in the eyes, we will recognize that our faith is what we challenge each and everyday. Too many seek spiritual teachings and learn to talk the talk and fear to surrender their ego to commit to the choices made long ago. Has it not been said that if your faith be that of a mustard seed you can do anything? Yes, do stand tall and look the Light in the eye and say thank you God for the privilege to have the freewill to plan and choose my fate. May you have the faith to build a strong foundation to trust your God self to walk the talk, talk built on divine truth and unconditional love. How you love yourself is how you love others and God. We are all one.

Now, with many years of experience in teaching and private practice David has invited his companion, friend, fellow teacher and wife, Richelle, to bring her sensitivity and insight to this revised and expanded Third Edition.

Richelle's spiritual journey began in high school when the traditional "truth" no longer served her understanding of life, and she redefined her values and truths to be more in alignment with her own heart. In college at U.C. Davis as a pre-medical biological sciences major, she ventured into the initial phases of spiritual studies by learning to meditate, practicing yoga and exploring whole foods nutrition. After graduation from college, she was not yet sure if she really desired to be a doctor of allopathic medicine, having the feeling inside her Higher Self, there was something yet to understand. This led to Richelle taking a year posting in Rockaway, New York, with the Marianist Voluntary Service Communities. Her volunteer work encompassed overseeing the medical needs of foster children in New York City and Long Island.

During this year her life would change as the small inner voice was answered. Through a newfound friend at St. John's Home and School for Boys where the volunteers lived, she was exposed to the teachings of Reiki. Her first exposure came about desiring to know about fasting. Her friend, a student of David's, put her copy of *Reiki Plus Natural Healing* in her hands. Drawn to the teachings contained in the book beyond the section on Fasting and Reiki Slaw, she read the book from beginning to end. This led to further discussions with her friend and the desire to study Reiki healing.

Richelle met David on March 16th of 1993, and began studying the healing system she had read about in his first book. Over the next several years she pursued her studies in the curriculum of the RPI. Although still in quandary about her life's path, Richelle returned to California to prepare for taking the MCAT to seek acceptance to medical school. Richelle was successful and attained invitations to four medical schools by December 1995, but requested a deferral for one year. During this year she traveled with David, co-teaching *Reiki Plus* classes in the

USA and Greece. At the conclusion of this deferral she realized that she was no longer aligned with the allopathic concept, and bridging the diametrically opposed philosophies of Western medicine and natural healing was beyond her heart's desire. Richelle declined her acceptance to Dartmouth medical school and devoted her life to teaching natural healing.

Richelle has devoted her energy full time to the shared teaching and management of the RPI with her husband David and is a Certified Natural Health Professional. She applies her knowledge of nutrition, iridology and herbs to an active healing practice.

An Unfolding Transition of Reiki: Philosophical Choices

If you are currently a student of Reiki you may find differences in healing concepts and philosophy taught by your Teacher. The intent of this book is to support and expand your understanding of Reiki; your practice and use of the sacred healing energy; and, to help establish a spiritual integrity and holistic platform of professionalism for Reiki. The authors are in no way interested in creating a dogmatic controversy, nor a conflict between the multitudes of doctrines and philosophies, that have sprung up around the teaching of Reiki, since the transition of Hawaya Takata on December 11, 1980.

We have attempted to present in this book the teachings passed down from Dr. Usui to Dr. Hayashi, from Hayashi to Takata, and from Takata to the teachers she trained. You will find in this text two approaches to Reiki Second Degree: the basic concepts taught by Takata to David's teachers, Virginia Samdahl, Barbara McCullough, and Takata's granddaughter Phyllis Furumoto, and the concepts of *Reiki Plus.* Where it is possible to distinguish the differences between the teachings, it will be so noted. We ask the reader to keep in mind that David's healing work covers a broad spectrum of experience and knowledge, as well as professional approaches in his private practice. Where it is appropriate, David is including this information with the hope that his experiences will provide insight to the reader, and reduce the learning curve.

So often we are asked, "What is standard Reiki procedure and what is not standard Reiki procedure?" In many situations to answer these questions presents a conflict of interest and the potential for judgment. Neither judgment nor conflict is of interest to us. However, what is of interest to us is that the teachings of Reiki be followed for the preservation of their sacred value and the continuation of their sacredness on the spiritual planes of manifestation. This, therefore, means not to adulterate the purity and sacredness of the Reiki energy through any distortion involving non-sacred association to the astral and other non-spiritual planes of manifestation, philosophies or practices lumped under a myriad of practices in the genre of metaphysical healing or studies. I Am Consciousness is the benchmark of *Reiki Plus* and for some teachers of Reiki. The meaning of Reiki is "The Spiritual Power of God." The teachings of Buddha and Jesus follow the same truths for the spiritual I Am Soul development.

The authors admire the teachings of the late Dr. Emmett Fox, a spiritual teacher and minister who transitioned in the fifties. His writings and teachings of divine metaphysics are a direct parallel to the philosophy we teach. Dr. Fox clearly distinguishes the differences between metaphysics and divine metaphysics in his books. Divine metaphysics is a clear and direct lineage of principles and teachings that has descended from the divine spiritual teachings of the ascended masters of the Brotherhood of Light. It does not embrace the dark arts or the psychic aspects of the energies present in the ethers of undeveloped souls. The focus of divine metaphysical teachings and practices is the development of the spiritual powers of sight and senses from the "non-attached ego conscious: use of these gifts to assist an individual's soul in its spiritual growth. It might interest the reader to know that Dr. Fox was invited by Charles and Edna Filmore to participate in the founding of the Unity Church. He declined this invitation because his personal ministry in Chicago was his focus, but his philosophy and books are a part of the foundation of Unity's ministry.

The authors have drawn into their soul's knowledge the inspiration of the pure teachings of those who have formed the thoughts of many: C. W. Leadbeater, Annie Besant, Corinne Heline, Kahlil Gibran, Cyril Scott, George Lamsa, Alice Bailey, Neville and Dane Rudhyar to mention only a few.

Statement of Intent

When a person is initiated into Reiki he is provided an opportunity to elevate his spiritual integrity. It is a personal choice to use his freewill to attain spiritual integration into his everyday life by transforming his ego. To surrender the "little wills of men"[1] to allow "Thy will be done, not mine" is the humbling challenge facing man's attunement with his I Am higher consciousness.

It is the specific intent of *Reiki Plus* to provide the ethical parameters, a spiritual foundation and a high quality of professional training to each student pursuing Reiki. We hope you succeed in becoming the holistic Practitioner you dream of in your heart of hearts. We realize that there are many avenues and choices of study under the

[1]Alice A. Bailey, The Great Invocation, Lucis Trust

title of Natural Healing and Reiki. If you so choose to pursue your studies with us, know that we are here for the Seventh Generation, dedicated to excellence in the field of natural healing and to the professional training of our students.

Not only will you learn the multifaceted dimensions of healing, you will be personally inspired to continually develop and evolve your spiritual foundation into the parallel realm of your human temple. The reward of bringing the I Am higher consciousness into everyday life is beyond anyone's description other than your own personal radiant smile of God's unconditional love and forgiveness flowing through you for all to see, feel and share.

A Time for Second Degree

Initiation has been discussed in David's first book *Reiki Plus Natural Healing*. However, what was not taught to many teachers of Reiki is the time period needed between initiation into the First Degree and Second Degree level of energy. The minimum time period between these two degrees is three months. Why is there a need to wait between each degree? Let's explore a variety of factors involved in initiation.

The reason for the period of three months between First and Second Degree is to allow the student's body time to integrate the changes that are created by the four initiations given by a Reiki Master in First Degree. The entire physiological and subtle body complex undergoes alteration of its biomagnetic energy. This energy brings about massive changes for many students. The first twenty-one days of the initiation process are dynamic for all students of Reiki, whether it is their initiation into First or Second Degree Reiki.

Unresolved issues or physical imbalances that exist prior to initiation often determine the specific dynamics of emotional, physical and mental changes experienced. From this perspective alone, proper evaluation of a student's readiness for initiation to the Second Degree level of Reiki is necessary by the teacher.

Third Degree Practitioner Initiation

Third Degree Practitioner level initiations in the *Reiki Plus* system require a Second Degree student who has practiced daily treatments on himself to wait at least six months before he is considered for evaluation by his teacher to be initiated to this level. Most students wait a year or more. The reason why is simple. The transformation invoked by the Third Degree initiation can require up to one year to integrate. Mastership initiation presents challenges beyond the scope of this book. Even the years a Third Degree Practitioner spends in training for Mastership in the Usui and *Reiki Plus* Systems will not exclude the new teacher from major personal and spiritual life transformations.

Takata's Second Degree Training

The training and initiation into Second Degree Reiki as passed down by Takata is simplistic. Second Degree in the Usui tradition is primarily an energy increase to be applied to the technique of First Degree, along with learning a simple system of absent healing.

Once David had learned the sacred symbols of Second Degree, which he did privately, his initiation and training by Virginia Samdahl lasted for approximately thirty minutes. In her loving and yet seriously playful manner, Virginia told him to go and apply what he had been given, and learn from the experiences that would be provided by his clients. In doing so, David incorporated his years of etheric body healing experience, spiritual training in divine metaphysics and Reiki healing sessions to develop his use of Reiki.

Reiki Plus Second Degree

The Second Degree class spans eight to sixteen hours of training. The class is normally taught over a two-day period or divided into evening modules. All students of Reiki are welcome to take Second Degree. If you have not read *Reiki Plus Natural Healing* Fourth Edition you will find it to be a companion text. Any Reiki student or teacher who wishes to be granted credit for Second Degree in the *Reiki Plus* Practitioner's Program, must also complete the training in *Reiki Plus* First Degree. This can be accomplished by attending the seminar or taking the seminar through our Home Study Program.

A Second Degree Reiki student may take *Psycho-Therapeutic Reiki Plus* without taking *Reiki Plus* First or Second Degree. In this seminar you will be taught the *Psycho-Therapeutic* technique of healing, portions of this material is found in Chapter Six in this book. This course is the foundation of the *Reiki Plus* System of Natural Healing and is a prerequisite for certification as a *Reiki Plus* Practitioner. The Home Study Course includes the study manual and audiocassette tapes.

Chapter 1

Second Degree Healing Energy

Second Degree Reiki is an entirely different vibrational energy than First Degree. First Degree is warm and gently radiates out of the entire hand. Your integration of the Second Degree energy will parallel your acclimation to the flow of First Degree energy you experienced.

Second Degree is an intense beam of energy shooting from the palm of the hand, also known as the palm chakra. A unique phenomena that occurs is the more you use Second Degree the more defined the palm chakra becomes. It is clearly a distinct circle of flesh colored skin surrounded with a pinkish to red flesh colored skin – almost as though the capillary blood has been reduced due to the intense flow of the Reiki energy.

As you begin your exploration into this new and exciting vibration of healing energy, let go of considerations that Second Degree will just be more of the same type of energy. Since energy is primarily kinesthetic, you will then be privileged to the unique experience of personally learning how it feels when it flows out of your hands.

Pay close attention to the variances of temperatures each hand will experience; often the palm and the back of the hand will send a different message to the brain, so do not be surprised. Further variances in temperature occur between what you feel and what is felt by the client. You may have the feeling of coolness in your hands and yet the client may be experiencing heat emanating from your hands. This phenomenon occurs as a cooling effect on the back of your hand, while the palm side is sending immense amounts of energy into the client.

The energy is often experienced in reverse, where the hand is cool to the client and yet, feels hot to you. In this occurrence the imbalanced energy is being pulled or extracted from the client. This does not mean that the imbalanced energy or pain is being extracted by you personally. Magnetic healing is not aligned with the principles of Reiki, due to the inherent dangers to the healer. Remember that Reiki has innate intelligence and therefore gives or takes energy according to the client's need to establish balance to the body.

Your hands and possibly your arms will also go through an adjustment period as the channels through which the Reiki Energy flows open wider. Energy flows through the cardiovascular system, the muscles and the physical-etheric body, the first etheric body. During the *Twenty-One Day Initiation* period the passageways are established and stabilized.

The *Twenty-One Day Initiation* period will provide a deeper and broader insight for your desired expansion of consciousness and the challenges presented by your progression through the Rays (see Chapter Six). The opportunities presented during your three cycles through the Rays, clearing each chakra twenty-one times, requires focused attention for you to gain the highest potential for personal growth and spiritual insight. It has been said by some esoteric and Zen schools that it requires at least twenty-one years to attain Mastership of any study. This knowledge of self mastery through the Rays is a minimal period of twenty-one years. The completion of the Rays of the Personality is only the graduation from "high school" so to speak, as it is during this time period that the soul communicates to the ego the lessons that must now be transformed to actually gain spiritual soul level consciousness. There are Twelve Rays for human consciousness to integrate in a lifetime. The Eight through Twelfth provide the soul opportunities for changing the emotional DNA imprint of the current incarnation. By changing the emotional DNA imprint the ego releases its need to have the lesson again, therefore the lesson becomes a positive attribute for the soul's next expansion of understanding.

Characteristics of the Energy Forms called Symbols

The energy forms of Reiki Second Degree are not all symbols. Of the three energy forms, two are symbols and one consists of Japanese Kanji, which spell out a statement. The Empowerment Symbol and the Mental-Emotional Healing Symbol are symbols of sacred geometry. The Absentia energy form is Japanese writing. Many Reiki teachers stylize the five Kanji characters of Absentia into what they called the "twenty-two mystical strokes", which then look like a Japanese Chit, to invoke the power of the Absentia healing energy. A Japanese Chit is a stylized combination of characters to represent the name of a person, however each character is properly written, which is not the case with the twenty-two mystical strokes.

Differences exist between the three individual energy forms of Second Degree. Where the Empowerment Symbol, which turns on the energy of second degree, is independent, the energy forms symbolizing Absentia and Mental-Emotional Healing are dependent. They are dependent upon the energy of the Empowerment Symbol to activate and to initiate their individual energies through time and space. Each of these will be thoroughly discussed in each section on these energy forms.

The Symbols of Second Degree

The symbols used in Second Degree Reiki are sacred and therefore not included in this book. Students who become initiates of Second Degree are charged with the responsibility of retaining and maintaining these mystical secrets.

Misuse of sacred mysteries seems to bring a dilution of energy and an eventual loss of understanding to the irreverent party. History has always proven this to be true. Mystical truths passed down from generation to generation and from civilization to civilization have been lost when used for personal power and greed or with the lack of spiritual integrity.

In the past thirty years the teachings of mystical and esoteric truths have become widespread, because more souls are ready for higher consciousness. To be entrusted with sacred knowledge bears the responsibility to use it with respect. It is our hope that human consciousness is not, once again, harmed by the desires of the human ego for personal power. The heart must be the guide for each soul to attain the consciousness of unconditional love. This progressive and exponential expansion of consciousness is aided by each person's understanding of the principles of Freedom through Responsibility.

Let each of us will the will of spirit and use our ego power to surrender the little wills of men. Only by doing so will we empower the 21st Century and the Aquarian Epoch in peace and accord. Peace is first to be established in each person. This is the union of the selves, undivided and therefore a Trinity. It is the union of the two selves that is meant when Jesus said, "When two are gathered together in my name, I AM present." Reiki is first for self-healing, which is where our true journey on the path began and must continue. Is this not what Paul meant when he said, "Physician, heal thyself?" Let us follow this lead with Reiki as a guide to expand our consciousness of unconditional love and awaken our God- Self. Using Reiki everyday to treat yourself is one key to unlocking this potential – for it is an act of unconditional love to give yourself a Reiki treatment.

Life is a healing process. Each day provides an opportunity to learn, understand and hopefully gain wisdom. Reiki is a wonderful tool to assist in this healing experience called life.

The Empowerment Symbol

The Empowerment Symbol is an independent energy form. It stands alone, requiring no other energy symbol to initiate its energy into action, or to function and move through time and space. The color of Second Degree energy is golden, surrounded by an energy field of emerald green. Gold is the vibration of the Eighth Ray and is the color emanated from God: the divine radiation of unconditional love. Gold is the vibration of the sun and the solar logos.

The Second Degree symbol is used to bring the Reiki Second Degree energy into you, so it can flow through you and out of your hands. You must always turn on the Second Degree energy to channel it into you or a client. Unless the Empowerment Symbol is appropriately placed and the sacred words nonverbally recited, you will be channeling First Degree Reiki energy.

Activation of the Second Degree Energy Symbol

We must say a few words about the general approach used in this ritual, which are contrary to the standard teachings of Reiki as handed down by Hayawaya Takata. The *Reiki Plus* approach to activate the energy does not include the drawing of the Empowerment Symbol over the body of our client. It is our opinion that to do so invites too many questions by the client or persons not initiated into the sacred energy of Second Degree. The Spiritual Integrity of Reiki (SIR) is of supreme importance. We feel that to make any public use of the symbols is a direct violation of responsibility and integrity on the part of the individual. It implies a lack of respect of all sacred teachings on the part of the teacher and student. A true student of the mystical truths hold sacred all sacred teachings, whether they have been passed down by Dr. Usui and his disciples who carry on his healing ministry or from spiritual sources "who guide the little wills of men".

Visualization to Activate Second Degree Energy

The Empowerment Symbol is always visualized and projected with the mind's eye. Then the sacred words are intoned silently. Feeling, intent and mental out-picturing of the Empowerment Symbol and sacred words connect the healer with the healing energy of Second Degree Reiki.

Intoning

Intoning is the use of intent to empower sound with spiritual intent. This results in a higher vibrational energy, which has greater penetrating ability due to its increased magnitude. So when you nonverbally intone the sacred words, you are to do so with reverence and spiritual feeling.

If you have ever sung, or heard sung, the inspired choral compositions of the German composers, you know the feeling of the words "to intone feeling". You may have heard or sung the rounds of the "Om", or chants of the Franciscan Monks. The resonance of the tone reverberates through your entire body. It is all a matter of emotional participation.

The Second Degree Initiation sets the student's energy template for matching this vibrational frequency of this energy. So the intensity of the incoming energy of the Second Degree is therefore dependent upon your intent to physically embody the vibration of the sacred and divine energy held in the ethers. For our act of visualization and intoning with the mind's eye and voice is the manifestation of energy matter from meta-matter. The energy of Second Degree is always existing in the metaphysical plane of energy surrounding the earth. Your process is to consciously align your energy field as a receiver with this parallel energy plane. Each time you visualize the Symbol and intone the sacred words of this ritual to activate Second Degree, you do so from the vibrational rate that you yourself are capable of vibrating.

All persons have not created themselves equal. All persons are given the divine right to heal, however, some have a more natural gift than others due to their spiritual soul development – or you could simply call it one's unique and natural gift. Some people draw better than others, and others can play the piano and some people create masterpieces from the ethers. So it is with healing. Fortunately, it is a proven fact that all can attune to the healing energy of Reiki and all persons willing can refine their vibrations through spiritual practice and meditation. Wherever you reside in this spectrum of light, know that practicing healing on the self everyday removes the particles of fear held in the energy field by one's ego investment. So, accumulate the dividends of spiritual wealth and give yourself a Reiki treatment each and everyday.

Empowering the Chakra Bodies

This technique of empowering the chakra bodies with the Second Degree energy is taught in the Second Degree Class of *Reiki Plus*. To present it within the text would be disrespectful to the Sacredness of the teachings of Reiki. Just consider that the manner that we "turn on" Second Degree balances and harmonizes the chakra bodies. The value of this technique is that the alignment of the chakra bodies temporarily removes emotional and/or mental fragmentations. In other words, turning on Second Degree in this manner will center you, balance you and bring you into immediate focus. It will likewise assist you if you meditate in this energy to gain understanding of why the fragmentation exists, and what lessons are being presented to you in your life.

Empowering the Back of your Hands

Once the energy has been empowered into the Etheric Bodies and is circulating through your physical body, it is necessary to direct the Reiki energy out of your hands. This may be done in one of several ways. First, you acknowledge your ability to visualize, whether you prefer two- or three-dimensional visualization on the hands does not matter. Then visualize the Empowerment Symbol over each hand individually or collectively over both hands.

The Invocation and Prayer

The vibration of intoning unites the healer and client with the spiritual essence of the consciousness of unconditional love, to guide both the client and the Practitioner in the healing. Intent is the key ingredient for preparing the healer to surrender to the will of God and the will of the client. Healing is always "Thy will be done, not mine."

The verbal prayer, when intoned with resonance and intent, aligns the healer and client with a focus upon the divine healing. Healing for the highest soul purpose of the client requires his participation. The prayer presents to the client your seriousness and his responsibility to surrender his fears of knowing the truth to the unconditional love and forgiveness of God. The client must open his heart to be worthy to receive and to do his work honestly. If he does, then the healing is 100 percent. The continued expansion of awareness increases the psycho-emotional health of the client to reach his goal of wellness.

Hand Positions on the Body

The hand placements for a Second Degree Reiki treatment are the same positions used in a First Degree Reiki treatment. The sequence of hand placements always begins with Position #1 on the face and continues with the remainder of the Head positions. Then treat the Torso and Back of the recipient. The legs of the client should always be treated during the first session to check the physical balance of the muscles, bones and nerves.

Remember that old injuries will need balancing, even though they have quit sending messages through the central nervous system to the brain or radiating pain. This is due to the memory stored in the tissue, what we call somatic or tissue memory. This is discussed more thoroughly in Chapter Six.

The time needed to balance each part of the body is different between First and Second Degree. Treatment time is reduced. This is the result of the Second Degree energy penetrating deeper into the soma and out into the chakra bodies. This provides a rapid elimination of pain and discomfort throughout the healee's body. When the discomfort of the body is reduced and eventually eliminated, balance of the bodies begins to be re-established. So the subtle and dense bodies are equally affected by the Second Degree energy.

As you change treatment positions on the body, you are in effect touching the body, as if for the first time. We find that with each hand placement on our bodies, or the body of a client, we desire to establish a special bonding. This bonding is accomplished by re-empowering our hands after placing them in the new position. This re-empowerment procedure is not necessary to insure that the Second Degree energy is given to each body position. However, the act of re-empowering provides a special blessing to the body part and creates a direct bond with each cell and organ. The experience is most rewarding. It is a mystical union which words are unable to express.

As you work with Second Degree you will establish your own understanding about its unique and variable attributes, and how the innate intelligence of Reiki directs the healer who is open to listening to his intuitive faculties. What you have learned from your training and practice with First Degree Reiki will be the platform from which you will learn to build and integrate an enhanced, deeper use of Second Degree energy.

The Reiki Treatment

Self Treatments

A student of Reiki who has given herself a daily treatment can expect that it will now take about 20 - 25 minutes to complete a maintenance treatment. This is a saving of approximately 35 minutes a day. If you have an active physical imbalance or emotional challenge, your treatment will be longer than stated. You will establish balance faster than you did using First Degree energy because the energy penetrates the cell more intensely.

Multiple Empowerments

The empowerment of Second Degree energy can be called forth over and over while treating a specific body part. This increases the quantity of Second Degree energy into a deficient organ, chakra center or injured part of the healee's body. Each empowerment must be completed before initiating another. You will find that deficient areas quickly fill up with healing energy and reach balance. This type of tissue or organ can be looked at visually like you are filling up the space occupied by an upside down mushroom, where the energy spreads out through the space of the organ or surrounding tissue.

Who Needs a Reiki Treatment

We must not lose scope that the Reiki treatment is not just for someone suffering from pain or emotional trauma. The beauty of Reiki is that it brings balance to all living energy systems. Our life is constantly filled with daily tasks and stress that deplete the vital energy from the biomagnetic energy field and the physical body. Reiki is a natural modality for a stress reduction practice.

If you are initiated into the energy of Reiki, you have the divine pleasure to give yourself a treatment daily or more often. The reasoning behind self-treatment is the same for a non-initiated Reiki person to consider receiving weekly or bimonthly treatments. The treatment eliminates stress and is a way to receive nurturing from another person, as well as enhance your emotional, mental and physical well being.

As a Reiki Practitioner do not limit your spiritual healing only to persons who are suffering from an illness or emotional crisis. Let your potential clients know that receiving a weekly Reiki treatment is parallel to receiving a massage. If you are a massage therapist, be sure that your clients are aware that they are receiving two gifts at once, and remember to turn on the Second Degree before starting the massage.

Treating Others

When you treat others, the time period will reduce to approximately 45 minutes to 1 hour. Of course, if your client has an acute or longstanding chronic imbalance it may take longer. We suggest that you allow space between clients if you schedule them in blocks of time. Fifteen minutes between clients allows for the unexpected extension of a session due to any client's special needs. It also offers you a break between healings to rest, cleanse the room, and psychologically prepare for your next session.

Since Reiki is a spiritually based healing process, initiating the reversal of energy from imbalanced to balanced energy, the individual's state of mind, body, and emotions must be attuned to the process of healing. Not only is the client directly involved in the healing process, he must be made aware that he is the true healer.

To bring the energy of the healee's body to a higher state of harmony, treat the entire body three days in a row. Three days are normally required to take the client up through the healing curve into the escalation of wellness where cellular and spiritual regeneration begins to gain ground. The body's energy is stimulated, re-establishing the function of the organs and endocrine glands affected by the illness. Treatments are continued on a scheduled basis until energy production of the body is self-generating. Eventually treatment will be spaced from weekly to biweekly, then monthly, until the client is totally capable of maintaining a balanced energy pattern without trauma when confronted with the challenge instigating the need for the healing work.

Stress and Reiki

Balance is the key to eliminating life's stress. Understand that each individual is totally responsible for creating either a positive or negative approach to stress. When the awakening of this understanding is sparked in each of us, we become capable of transmuting our self-created states of stress to inner peace, and the feeling of being centered takes place. Imbalanced energy is the emotional by-product of stress. Improperly channeled, it leads to a loss of the individual's clear perspective of life. Holding unbalanced energy within the individual's mind, body, and emotions leads to a state of unwellness, which manifests itself as symptoms of physical or mental illness.

Spiritual perception is a conscious acceptance of Truth. This awareness leads an individual to understand the multifaceted aspects involved in the physical and emotional states of unwellness, including the willingness to take responsibility and admitting that the "I" of "my ego" is limiting harmony. Clarity of thinking is required for eliminating the many aspects involved in this state of imbalance. Unless the individual is willing to approach the illness in this manner, a total healing may never be achieved. It is by treating the whole person with their direct participation that the illness is reversed to a state of harmony, balance, and emotional well-being.

Reiki works on the physical and Etheric Bodies during the Reiki treatment. Energy is provided that awakens the inner consciousness of the client, without the necessity of counseling by the healer; however, if a Practitioner is trained in counseling then his training should be incorporated in his healing techniques.

There are many daily exercises an aspiring healer will find to be an essential part of their day. We have found giving oneself a daily full-body Reiki treatment and remembering the Five Spiritual Principles to be very worthwhile. Over the years of teaching, our students have heard us say, "If you serve yourself Reiki everyday, it will serve you." Reviewing the Spiritual Principles and allowing the breadth of their meaning into the daily process of your life will allow you to begin to master the ego challenges you will face. You will grow spiritually and your perception will expand into the hologram of truth. As this occurs gently, one day at a time, so will you heal your life's challenges. You will hear God's truth within your own heart when your mind is at peace.

Putting words into action is a most important step in healing. Since life is a continuous act of healing ourselves, we must acknowledge our chosen challenges for growth.

Action is the energy of imagination;
Imagination is the energy of thought;
Thought is the energy from the Divine Source of God.

The direction of this thought energy is dependent upon the choice of the individual for love and wellness, or the blocking of love, creating illness.

By healing the physical body the client can then direct his energy to balancing the various aspects of the causal factor leading to a state of illness. In all healing, the client must reach into the inner process of his consciousness and be willing to surrender to the truth, to become the healer. Self-healing confronts the validity of past choices and necessitates that the ego cast off the errors of old precepts of freewill. When the "I" can surrender, the divine self can begin to hear, feel and see clearly the path of choice God presents at this moment for enlightenment. This is your truth. It fills all dimensions of your physical and cosmic reality and it stretches your spiritual fabric. The opportunity may even turn you upside down on a path of action filled with temptations of resistance or any number of ways to challenge your truth. You must learn to be open and receptive to "Thy will be done, not mine." Let us remember that to be in the flow of life is to be nonresistant, to be open to all of God's gentle love and direction, wisdom and guidance, joy and laughter. Another factor of life and healing is that without chaos appropriately metered out by God, humankind cannot exercise freewill to understand that change is the needed elixir. This chaos is the universe teaching us that the statement "Thy will be done, not mine" is a truth of growth.

Post Treatment Procedure

Be sure to offer the client a glass of water to aid the clearing of the energy field and the physical body. Encourage the consumption of one-half the body weight in ounces per day, which is considered the amount needed by the body. We are referring to water without the chemicals of chlorine, fluorine and other toxic substances harmful to the healthy function of the body

Remember, if this is the first treatment, mention the Twenty-One Day Healing Cycle and the emotional, mental and physical responses that do occur. Each client will respond to healing according to his or her accumulated and current physical, emotional and mental challenges. Also consider the client's need for utilizing cleansing baths for detoxification of imbalanced emotional energy and pain.

This is a time to discuss the experiences and insights that came to the client's awareness during the treatment. Listening is the best approach. What you learn can help you clarify without analyzing or playing the role of "I know what is wrong" or being a psychic. The client is the only person who has his answers. A good healer is an effective listener.

You can assist in developing positive objectives by suggesting an Affirmation of Action for the week and offering a focus for the client's daily meditation. We also find it helpful to lend the client supportive reading material from our lending library, or suggest a book they can purchase at the local bookstore. You will have your favorites; however, the Reading List in Chapter Seven may prove useful. Try not to suggest a book that will stretch the client beyond his present ability to integrate the challenges currently in his life, or books that are contrary to his religious, philosophical, moral or social beliefs.

The speed of healing is greatest when it is gentle. Then the new awareness can be gradually integrated into the client's spectrum of reality. The time it takes for a client to reach his goals of wellness will be determined individually. The time an individual requires to regain balance and rebuild his body is unique to the nature of the person's challenges. We have observed that healing the holographic layers of the psyche, the body and the ego is a process of unlayering the four aspects of the mind: unassociated conscious memories, associated conscious memories, subconscious memories and collective unconscious memories. The effective healer learns to assist the individual's natural process slowly and gently. This gentle manner allows the lessons contained in the challenge can be more easily integrated to affect subtle changes in the body and psyche of the client.

One suggestion for healing is that the client work with the Lord's Prayer, because the eight verses correspond to the eight chakras:

8th	Mother-Father God
7th	who art in Heaven
6th	Hallowed be Thy Name
5th	Thy kingdom come, Thy will be done on Earth as it is in Heaven,
4th	Give us this day, our daily bread
3rd	and forgive us our trespasses as we forgive those who trespass against us
2nd	Lead us not into Temptation, but deliver Us from Evil
1st	Thine is the Kingdom and the Power and the Glory

Combine the Lord's Prayer with the Forgiveness Exercise will provide an avenue of spiritual healing on the physical plane. (See Chapter Seven on Forgiveness.) We highly recommend Sermon on the Mount, by Dr. Emmet Fox, (Harper and Row). In fact, we recommend all of Dr. Fox's books for they are treasures of divine light, as are the books of Neville (DeVorss).

Chapter 2

Distant Healing

Absentia, healing at a distance, is the act of making contact with a person who is not in your physical presence. The distance is not important, for time and space are nonexistent in spiritual reality. Spiritual reality is parallel to the union of the mystical trinity and the absence of duality.

There are no rigid rules, do's or don'ts governing the application. The only exception to this is to never use the Key (mental–emotional symbol) energy in Absentia [students completing the training given in the Psycho-Therapeutic Reiki Plus seminar, learn the dangers of this symbol and how to use it to always protect the psyche of the client]. Most persons begin to use the Absentia healing technique immediately. You may send healing at a distance as long as you feel comfortable.

Absentia is a direct contact through the mystical powers of the sacred words and symbols from the healer to the higher consciousness of the client. We are making contact with the Seventh Etheric Body, the Seventh chakra.

Absentia is governed by a divine law of healing, "Thy will be done not mine." This law translates to say that unless the client will consciously utilize the healing energy to increase his Light, the Reiki energy will not flow from your hands into him. We find that it does not matter whether the individual has asked or has not asked for the absent healing energy. It depends upon his conscious intent to qualify God's unconditional love for his personal healing. We can never lose sight of another divine law of healing: the client is the true healer, because the healer is only a facilitator for the client.

The First Precept of Reiki Healing governs in accordance with these divine laws: the asking must be sincere. If the energy does not flow from your hands when you empower the absentia characters, the client's Higher Self is speaking to you. It is saying his lower desire consciousness will not utilize the energy for his highest good; and, he is not ready to change his present consciousness, perception and vibrational energy level. Do not be disappointed. Do not allow your ego to get involved. The client is not open to change at this time. It is his freewill choice to continue as he is now. If you become emotionally involved or angered at his resistance, simply bless both of you and surround each of you with unconditional love, forgiveness and light. When the time is right (divine time), his freewill shall desire to reunite with his Higher Consciousness, and no longer have the desire to be lonely and separate from God's promise to humankind: be one with God

Basic Requirements for Treating

The client needs to ask you directly or to ask another person to ask you; and there needs to be some form of exchange. Do not charge when you feel that an equal exchange currently exists. This may include family, friends and students, whether requested orally or over the etheric wavelengths (when you hear in your "mind's ear").

Absentia is an excellent tool to promote and monitor the healing process of your clients. To assist a friend or family member in a crisis, you can set up a network of Second Degree healers to provide healing and emotional and physical support throughout the day.

It is appropriate to charge when no exchange exists at the time a person asks for the absent healing. This especially applies to a person requesting a series of healings for a specific condition and who is incapable of coming to you for treatment.

Absent healing for complex psycho-physical disorders requires uninterrupted concentration and takes 30 minutes to an hour to complete. This technique is taught in *Psycho-Therapeutic Reiki Plus* and further necessitates the client knowing what he must do during the absent treatment. Otherwise an absent treatment can be sent in a shorter period of time.

Schedule for treatments: A Professional Relationship

If a client is in an acute stage, then treatment for three consecutive days is required to move him through the healing curve crisis presented in Chapter Three of this book and Chapter Five of *Reiki Plus Natural Healing*. Schedule treatments according to the progress of the client once they are asymptomatic of pain. Chronic imbalances will vary; however, it is a good idea to anticipate not less than three consecutive treatments, with a total of seven to ten sessions.

We suggest that if you accept a client who will be treated solely by Absentia, you have him commit to no less than seven treatments. Payment in advance is common practice.

A Pre-counseling Interview needs to be included in your treatment time and the Healing Contract signed by both parties. Phone contact must also follow the sessions to keep you apprised of the client's opinion of his progress. If the call is long distance, ask the client to call you.

Distant Healing Procedure

Making contact with the person is called attuning to your client. If you do not know the individual, several facts are needed to effectively make contact with the client:

Name.
Picture—for non-visual persons, this aids your attunement.
Location—optional.
Medical or emotional challenge—optional and very helpful.

Writing the Absentia Kanji Characters and the Empowerment Symbol on the healee's face:

1. Visualize or feel the person in front of you. On his face you will write the sacred words. You may enlarge the size of the face to provide a larger surface for writing.
2. With your mind's eye write the Kanji characters of Absentia on the healee's face. You place the first character on the Third Eye and continue writing the characters down the face and the body if more space is needed (length and space is not critical).
3. Then non-verbally with your mind's voice, intone the sacred words of Absentia three times.
4. With your mind's eye write the Empowerment Symbol on top of the Absentia Symbol. Then, non-verbally with your mind's voice, intone the sacred words for Empowerment.
5. With the person facing you, place your hands on each side of the individual's head. Your right hand is on the person's left side and your left hand on his right side.
6. Reduce the symbols written on the face to a dot on the client's Third eye. Make a mental contact between your Third eye and the client's Third eye where the dot has been placed.
7. The mental contact, the mental act of intent to send distant healing, must be maintained throughout the healing, otherwise the energy will cease to be sent or received. If the energy becomes disconnected, simply repeat the steps above and resume the healing where you were on the body.

Registering Contact with the Healee

When contact is established energy is felt between the hands is felt. You are holding a ball of energy, a part of the etheric fabric of the healee's spiritual essence. You will physically sense the inability to bring your hands together, as long as the energy is transmitted to the client. This will continue throughout the healing as long as contact is maintained. If contact is lost, then the hands will be pulled together.

When an organ or muscle balances, the energy recedes like an "out breath" of tension, just as the magnetism decreases in a hands-on treatment. The hands are not pulled together. The sensation is like holding a spongy ball between your hands. There is resistance, but it is soft and fluffy.

The Reiki Plus System of Distant Healing

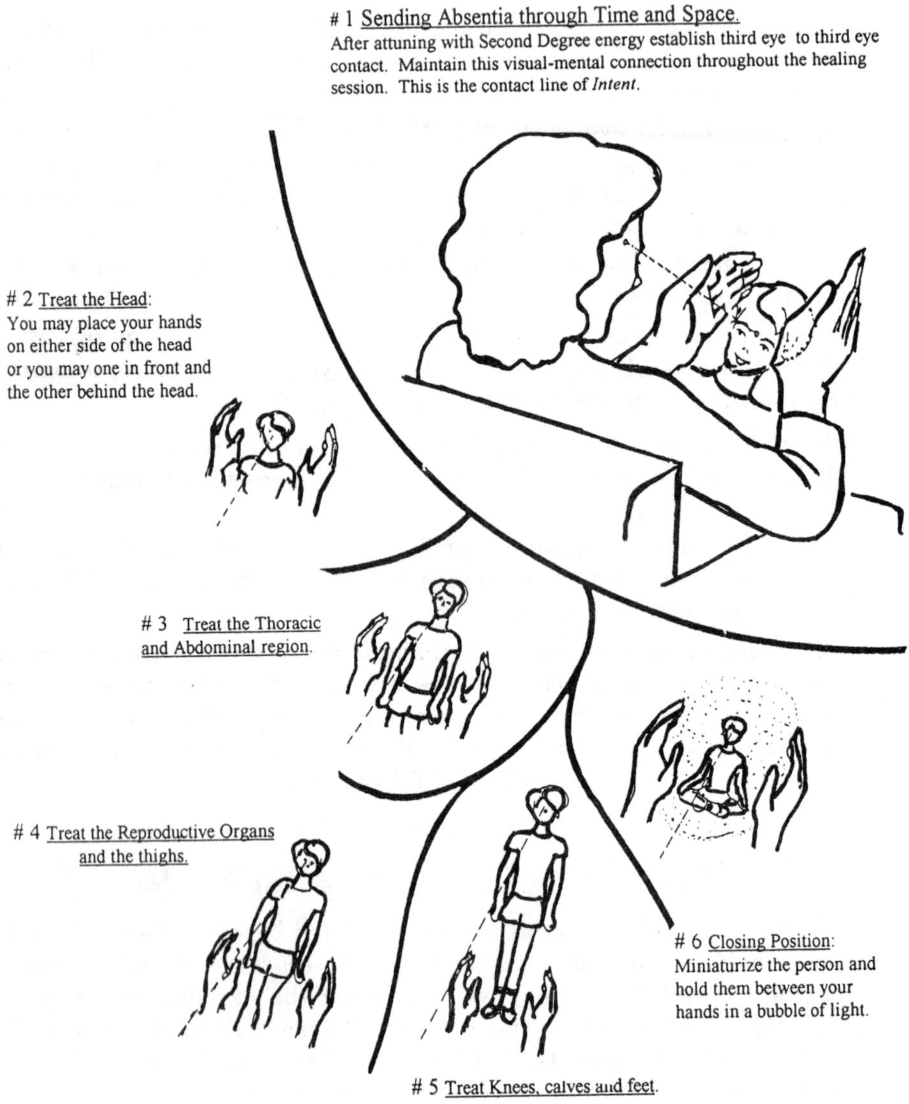

1 Sending Absentia through Time and Space.
After attuning with Second Degree energy establish third eye to third eye contact. Maintain this visual-mental connection throughout the healing session. This is the contact line of *Intent*.

2 Treat the Head:
You may place your hands on either side of the head or you may one in front and the other behind the head.

3 Treat the Thoracic and Abdominal region.

4 Treat the Reproductive Organs and the thighs.

5 Treat Knees, calves and feet.

6 Closing Position:
Miniaturize the person and hold them between your hands in a bubble of light.

Remember that your hands are sending energy to the organs, glands, muscles and skeleton. Each position collectively will need to balance before moving to the next area of the body. The fullness of the energy field experienced during the sending will soften when all body parts in a position are balanced, indicating that you can now move to the next sequenced position. If you work internally and expand the anatomical organ or body part, then be sure to balance the remaining part of the organ in that position before moving to the next position.

The Laser Beam Technique

This technique applies to Second Degree students of *Reiki Plus*, as their initiation is different than the standard Usui initiation. Their Third Eye is also initiated to facilitate Second Degree energy.

From your palm chakras and your Third eye you send a beam of Second Degree energy. The location is normally a specific part of the client's anatomy. You activate the laser beam by visualizing the Empowerment Symbol directed from each hand and Third eye into the anatomical part and complete the intoning of the sacred words. This empowerment gives additional healing energy specifically where it is directed.

If you are knowledgeable in gross anatomy, have specific diagnostic information about a client's health challenges, and are capable of detailed visualization, then you can work within the physical structure of an organ, gland, vascular or lymphatic duct, muscle, ligament or bone.

Selecting the Treatment

You may treat in several manners. One is the process of treating in a more detailed manner by anatomical subdivision, and the other is to treat the entire body at one time. Let's discuss these applications.

Full Body Treatment

You will be required to visually miniaturize the client to be the same size as your hands. This is the fastest method of sending Absentia. It is possible to see and feel hot spots on the body that indicate potential or known areas of imbalance or challenge. Remember, information you pick up is not for diagnostic purposes. Your hands will develop sensitivity and you will learn to recognize energy registration signifying imbalances in the client's body. If you are a sensitive person you may tune into the person's physical, emotional and mental needs.

Depending upon your perceptive abilities you may also receive input to the emotional and mental stress levels. Combine this with known factors given to you by the person. Make a mental record of the imbalances and the association of the chakra to organ groups. Write your findings in the client's file and verify with the client to establish the validity of your perceptions. Keep in mind that subtle energies registering from the Etheric Bodies may not be known or obvious to the client. If so, then the client may not be able to validate your perceptions. In such cases we suggest you use your *Physio-Spiritual Etheric Body* training to establish the origin of the energy imbalance, if you are a graduate of this seminar.

If you find a body part that will not balance, then use the Laser Beam Technique to expedite the healing. If you are trained in *Physio-Spiritual Etheric Body* healing, then use the techniques you learned in this training to fully balance the organ and chakra body of the client.

Masking

Masking occurs when one or more anatomical parts or subsections of an organ or gland needs more energy to balance than the entire anatomical part of the body covered by the hands. If this is happening, then another portion of the anatomy will not register in your hands until the most deficient part is balanced. Allow each section you treat to reveal all masked parts of the anatomy needing specific attention.

An example might be that of a person suffering from stress and fatigue. You might find the body having a conversation with you, as you are sending energy to the third chakra organ center, and all of a sudden you hear the Adrenals call out, "I am really depleted, please laser in on me and recharge my batteries." When they are balanced, the Liver might speak up and say, "The body has overloaded me with toxins, how about a little additional Reiki to clear me out?" Then when the Liver is happy, the Spleen might light up and say, "This stress has tired me out and the immune system needs strengthening before the body loses its ability to resist the emotional onslaught of a viral thought-form floating through its tired consciousness." So you take out time to fill up the Spleen until it smiles at you.

You continue to treat each body part until all layers within the anatomical section unmask and balance. Remember that even in Absentia the client will open to accept a deeper healing as each Etheric Body is balanced. Ultimately the energy you are experiencing is entering the client at the deepest cellular level within the physical body.

Absent Treatments by Subdivision of Anatomical Sections

Treatment by subdivision provides physical response in your hands as you contact each portion of the anatomy. The subdivision of the anatomy is in approximation to your hands placed vertically on the side, front or back of the body. Your hand is proportionate to the client's body you are treating. Please refer to the Sensory Registration Diagram later in this chapter.

Head and Neck: Pineal, pituitary, thalamus, hypothalamus, brain, optic nerves, eyes, ears (outer and inner sections to include the Eustachian tubes), the sinus cavities and nasal passages, the cranial bones; cervical vertebrae, spinal cord and nerves; oral-facial complex (mouth, tongue, throat, palate, etc.), thyroid and parathyroid, cervical section of the esophagus and larynx; the internal and external carotid arteries and jugular veins; the lymph glands of the head and neck; the bones, muscles and skin.

Upper Thoracic Region: Thymus, trachea, lungs, thoracic section of esophagus, heart and major arteries (aorta arch with branches to the carotid and vertebral, and the ascending, descending aorta; the pulmonary arteries; subclavian to the arms) and veins (superior and inferior vena cava and subclavian); the upper to mid thoracic vertebrae, spinal cord and nerves; the ribs and the arms (the humerus, radius and ulna are large bones which produce more white cells from the bone marrow for building the immune system); the lymph glands, especially in the upper thoracic region of breast and armpit area; the bones, muscles and skin.

Mid Thoracic to Upper Abdominal Region: The liver, the gall bladder, spleen, stomach, pylorus and duodenum, pancreas, adrenals, kidneys and ureters and transverse section of the large colon, the arterial and venus blood flow and mid to lower thoracic vertebrae, spinal cord and nerves; the lymph glands; the bones, muscles and skin.

Lower Abdominal and Reproductive Region: The small intestines (jejunum and ileum), the ileo-cecal valve/orifice, cecum and appendix, ascending and descending large colon, sigmoid colon, rectum, anal canal and anus; the ovaries, fallopian tubes, uterus, and vagina, or the penis, testes and prostate; the ureters, bladder and urethra; the lumbar vertebrae, spinal cord and nerves, and the pelvis, sacrum (root branch of sciatic nerve originates from the end of the central spinal cord) and coccyx; the common and internal iliac artery and vein; the lymph glands; the bones, muscles and skin.

Legs to Feet: Especially the larger leg bones—femur and tibia where more white cells begin their life for building the immune system; femoral artery and vein, the great saphenous vein and the veins and arteries of the lower legs and feet; the sciatic nerve and foot reflex points; the lymph glands; the bones, muscles and skin.

Closing the Distant Healing

The distant healing is closed by seeing the client miniaturized , while holding him between your hands. You encapsulate the individual in golden-white light. The golden-white light looks like a glorious illuminated halo of vibrant crystalline shimmers of liquid white mother-of-pearl with sparkles of gold floating through the depths and on the surface of the light. When the client is balanced, your hands will be magnetically pulled together. The touching of the fingertips breaks the energy connection.

If you need to end the Absent Healing session before the client's body has signaled completion or you have had time to send healing to each part of the body, simply visualize the client surrounded by the healing energy and release him. You are in fact sending the energy mentally forward in time allowing the client to continue receiving the energy.

Sensory Registration in Your Hands When Treating

This diagram denotes where energy registers in the hands if an energy imbalance exists in that specific area. This diagram is a guide and only applies to the hands being placed beside the head. If your hands are in front or behind the head, this diagram will not be valid. You will have to imagine the location of the organs concurrent with the position you are covering, e.g., Position #1 Head or Position #3 Back of the Head.

Only when the hands are holding the head in this manner, the thumb extends to the anterior centerline of the face and the little finger and edge of the palm extend to the posterior centerline of the occiput and cervical vertebrae. The numbered points on the hands refer to the following parts of the head:

1. crown chakra; 2. pineal gland; 3. pituitary gland; 4. left eye; 5. sinus cavities; 6. oral facial complex; 7. ear and auditory complex; 8. throat, thyroid gland; 9. occiput region, eyes, pulse rate, etc.; 10. cervical vertebra and any related function via neurological connection, neck muscles.

The amount of Reiki energy drawn from your hands will be specific to the amount needed to balance the area covered. You will experience the increase and decrease of magnetism and energy, the same as in hands-on healing. When a position is balanced, your hands will no longer transmit the energy as intensely. The energy ball becomes fluffy around the edges like a cotton ball, but still maintaining a fullness inside the energy field.

Refer to the CIBA Collection of *Medical Illustrations* by Frank H. Netter, M.D. and *Grant's Atlas of Anatomy,* by James E. Anderson, M.D. (Williams and Wilkins) offers further study and education of anatomy and anatomical parts covered by each specific Reiki position.

Takata's Standard Reiki Distant Healing

Takata taught a very nice and easy approach for the healer to send Reiki to another person. This system, we have to presume, was taught to her by Dr. Hayashi. He trained and initiated her in Reiki and later to Mastership on February 21, 1938 in Honolulu, Hawaii. The Healer uses a photograph of the client to write the Absentia Characters and the Empowerment Symbol on the person's face. The mental energy contact process must be maintained to keep the energy flowing.

Then using your right leg for the front of the client's body, from the knee to the hip, the healer places his hands side by side. First, the hands are placed with the fingertips at the knee and hands resting on the thigh. You will experience a rise and fall of the energy from your hands into your leg. After each hand placement has balanced, move upward to the top of the thigh. This completes treating the front of the client from the head to the toes. Then repeat the same procedure on the left leg for the back of the body.

Registering Contact With the Healee

When contact is established a fullness between the hands is felt. You are holding a ball of energy, a part of the etheric fabric of the healee's spiritual essence. You will physically sense the inability to close your hands, palm to palm, as long as energy is being received by the client. This will continue throughout the healing as long as contact is maintained. If contact is lost, then the hands will be pulled together.

When an organ or muscle balances, the energy recedes like an "out breath" of tension, just as the magnetism decreases in a hands-on treatment. The hands are not pulled together. The sensation is like holding a spongy ball between your hands. There is resistance, but it is soft and fluffy.

Sensory Registration in Your Hands When Treating the Head During Absentia

(See Page 34)

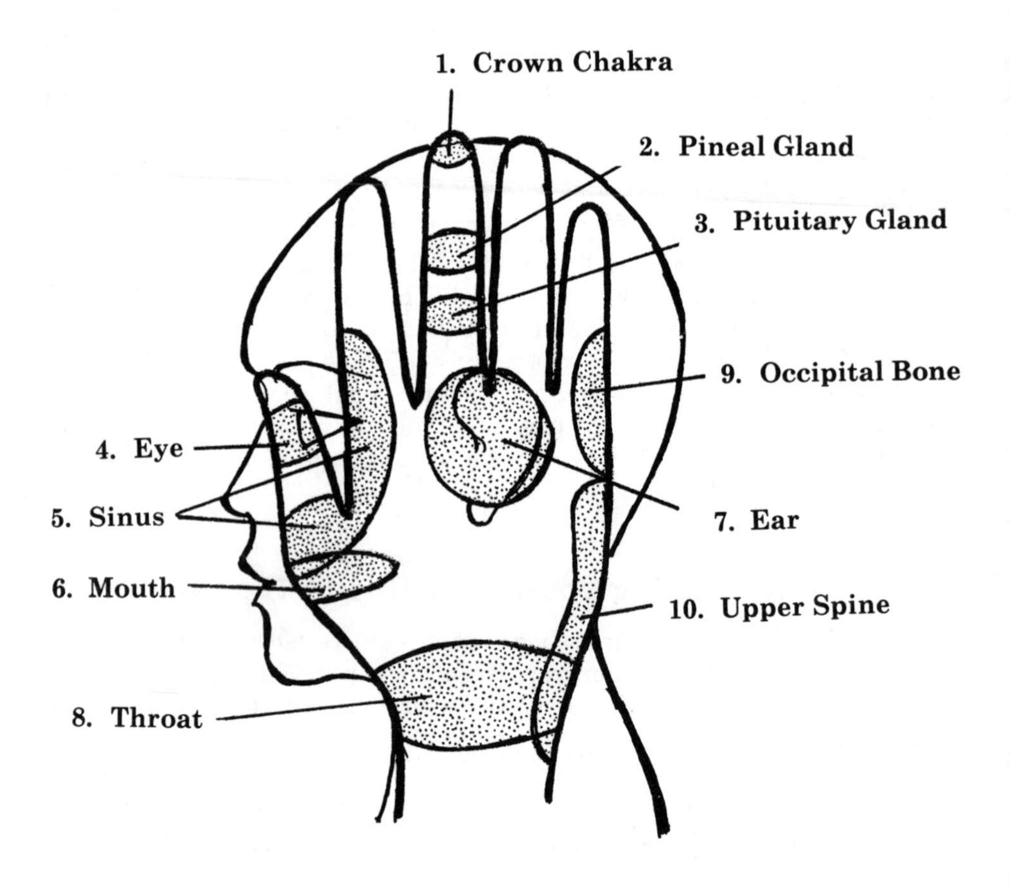

Chapter 3

Establishing a Professional Relationship

Our Model for Healing

Our thesis of healing is based upon the spiritual and karmic unfolding of freewill choice. There is an old adage that more or less states, good choices good consequences, bad choices bad consequences. We can even find reference in the Bible relating to, "what ye sow, so shall ye reap." However we wish to state this thesis, the bottom line is still the same. In direct parallel to this reality, we find that the results of freewill resulting in a negative impact upon the psyche builds a residual of emotional charge. This residual, if not dealt with effectively, will eventually create dysfunction of a chakra body. The result will in time effect the organ or body system the chakra body controls.

This brings us to the next factor, the ego's investment in holding on to the consequences and how it becomes the causal factor in a disease process. So let's take a look at the method by which a person can address her investment of ego to create a new pattern of understanding. How does an old choice play out to create an emotional, mental and physical imbalance? In our way of thinking, all physical and mental imbalances have an emotional basis as the root stimulation. The emotional body, the third chakra body, and the adrenal glands are in partnership with the sympathetic nervous system. Stress results from decisions of freewill choice, which result in negative stimulation to the psyche. The ego becomes attached to the invested energy of being right, or more importantly, does not want it proven that the ego chose poorly. So the result is what we term the emotional causal factor. The needed process is its proper release from our energy field.

The first step in this release of the emotional causal factor from the energy field is that the client must become aware that she is attached to the process. Only the individual can change this attachment, since it allows the continuation of the imbalanced pattern in the person's life. The attachment is the person's desire to have the same pattern continue in her life since the ego wishes to maintain the status quo and continues to hide behind it's fearful defenses. This desire or habit perpetuates the psycho-physical disorder.

It is imperative that the individual realizes that she is the actual cause of the condition and that she desires to have it on a soul level for her growth. In the manifestation of the psycho-physical disorder the person chooses to use the illness or emotional imbalance as a learning tool. It is from this perspective that the psycho-physical imbalance must be viewed.

Our philosophy accepts that the genetic choice for a given incarnation is appropriate for the challenges of the personality for soul growth. Does your client? You will need to learn to recognize where your client's beliefs are in relationship to this concept. If your client is not versed in divine metaphysics and the mystical teachings, you will need to convey this philosophy in the terminology she understands. The use of metaphysical words is not necessary, and most likely cannot convey this philosophy in an understandable format.

In many instances your client will not have prior awareness of the self-creation factor as the primary trigger of her challenges. Psycho-physical manifestations occur when an individual becomes separated from her feelings and intuition. This disassociation from one's inner knowing sets the stage for chaos to occur. We know that all stimuli register in the etheric bodies, simultaneously stimulating the chakra centers and the entire anatomy connected to the chakra centers. The psycho-physical disorders resulting from this avoidance and lack of personal responsibility by the client may require a longer healing process to correct.

Each client's level of personal awareness and acceptance of personal causality needs to be determined so the appropriate communication techniques are used to guide the healing process. The client who is consumed by fear and presents a victim-conscious perspective needs to be approached gently, with the Practitioner facilitating hands-on Reiki treatments in the beginning. As the energy of the Key is used over the course of several healing sessions, unconscious patterns and connections will begin to reveal themselves to the client who demonstrates her willingness to learn and grow. Conversely, the client who is in a centered space, and who accepts her freewill choices is ready to work on a deeper level than the client who is still consumed by victim-consciousness.

The Practitioner's Objectives

As the Practitioner, your objective is to supportively communicate the information the client is ready to hear. Your knowledge of her behavior patterns and experiences will be your reference point to begin communications and the healing work. You must clearly define steps that attune the client's conscious mind towards recognizing her old patterns, which will lead to the elimination of these old patterns. The Practitioner needs to be an effective listener and observer, which is necessary to convey clarity to the client.

The process of working with a client, to facilitate her healing, is best approached by first understanding that God sends people to you that you are capable of helping. Each client's case needs to be approached individually. You as the Practitioner will be a more effective facilitator the more you trust yourself and the more you trust God. Remember too, that often people will appear on your doorstep dealing with an issue or problem that you yourself have just been dealing with that very day or week. Any insight you have gained for yourself can be shared with the client. There is an adage that states "it's not the truth until you share it." In addition, your experience in the healing room will teach you how to deal with clients effectively. Be open to learn all that you can from each client in each healing session: were you effective in communicating; did what you share open a new door of understanding for the client; can you share your insights and guidance in more effective ways?

The Client's Responsibility to Attain these Objectives

The client must personally desire transformation in order to change the old patterns. She must desire to claim her own power to create effective results, and she must desire to reverse the stressful situations challenging her psycho-physical stability into positive learning experiences.

Components for Designing a Healing Agreement

A Healing Agreement acts like a contract between you and your clients. The agreement sets the tone for your relationship with the client and clearly states the boundaries of your healing relationship. As a professional Practitioner, the following guidelines should be followed in order to design a thorough healing agreement contract between you and your clients:

- The client's commitment to participate in the holistic approach of healing: treating the whole person physically, mentally, emotionally and spiritually.
- The client understands that active participation, cooperation and continuation of the healing process are necessary to reach her goal of wellness.
- The client agrees to make an equal exchange for the Practitioner's services.
- The client acknowledges that time is a requirement for sessions to show positive and progressive results.
- The client understanding that her progress is determined by how she deals with old thought patterns and habits.
- The client desires to forgive herself, the participant(s), and express gratitude to the participant(s) during the Forgiveness Meditation. (see Chapter Seven). The client can take steps towards this level of forgiveness through acceptance, releasing conflicting emotions, letting go

of intense feelings and letting go of her attachment to the internal turmoil related to the issue she is desiring to forgive.

- The Practitioner helps the client understand that holding on to feelings of guilt and sin maintain fear and doubt, anger and resentment, lack of self-worth, self-righteous judgment of self and others, and spiritual pride. This is only a partial listing of conflicting emotional patterns that can create life imbalances.

Any special conditions you discuss and agree upon can be added to the Healing Agreement in writing. If added by hand to your existing Agreement, be sure that you and the client initial the added conditions. You as the Practitioner can make no claim to heal diseases, to treat pathologies, make a diagnosis, prescribe medicines, herbs, or vitamins to treat a specific pathology or symptom. Never tell a client to refrain, cease or alter the intake of prescribed medications. You must maintain your clients' confidentiality and act with professional integrity with all information shared.

Ministry allows you to practice hands-on healing. It is still necessary for Natural Healers to carry Professional Liability Insurance. Ministry does not eliminate malpractice liability. The IMA Group, a nonprofit body workers organization offers liability insurance to Reiki Practitioners: PO Box Drawer 421, Warrenton, VA 20188 (540) 351-0800.

An Example of a Healing Agreement

The following is an example of a healing agreement or contract that you can use with your clients.

The client must make a commitment to participate in the healing process, which encompasses the holistic approach of treating the whole person physically, mentally, emotionally and spiritually.

The client affirms his or her understanding that the speed of healing and the number of sessions required to reach wellness is totally dependent upon the client. His or her faith, active participation and co-operation in the healing process are essential. The client agrees to make an exchange for the healing sessions.

The client also acknowledges that time is a requirement for the healing process to show positive and progressive results. The client understands that emotional and mental confrontations with the "old thought and habit patterns" will be a part of the healing process. How the client deals with each issue is of primary importance to the creation of physical, emotional, mental and spiritual well-being.

The client's acknowledgment of the act of forgiving self and the forgiveness of anyone he or she perceived to have caused his or her present growth opportunity is of instrumental importance. The direct participation by the client to release feelings of guilt and sin from his or her thought processes, be it directed at self or others, allows the client to initiate consciously the removal of fear and doubt the removal of anger and resentment, the removal of lack of self worth, and the removal of judgment of self and others.

Now in accordance with the healing procedure, both parties, client and the Practitioner, willingly agree to commit to one another his or her pledge to uphold his or her responsibility to achieve, to the best of their respective abilities all that is described in this Healing Agreement. This is a moral and ethical relationship for the spiritual healing of the client.

Goal of Wellness____

The client, ___________________________, fully accepts his/her responsibility in all life choices as acts of his or her personal freewill, to include but not limited to genetic selection and the creation of all of life's physical, mental, spiritual and/or emotional challenges (disease or dysfunction) now present in the client's life.

The client understands that the Practitioner is a spiritual facilitator assisting in the client's healing process; and the client acknowledges his or her full responsibility in achieving or not achieving the client's stated Goal of Wellness of his or her mind-body-spirit. The client desires to understand how to attain spiritual balance: a peaceful relationship with self and God. Spiritual healing is the objective of this healing process. The client understands that spiritual healing often stimulates hidden memories to surface during healings. Memories that surface present healing confrontations. If the client confronts and surrenders his/her ego choices that lead to the conflicts, the client will allow a healing of his/her mind-body-spirit. The client further acknowledges that healing is a process, a spiritual journey of life; and that healing is not always the restoration of physical wellness, the removal of symptoms or elimination of the cause. It is hopeful the client will achieve the understanding of why he or she needed this challenge in this lifetime.

Agreed upon rate of exchange per healing session $______

Client's Name:____

Client's Signature___________________________________ date_________

Practitioner's Name:____

Practitioner's Signature_____________________________ date________

Interviewing the Potential Client

The objective in interviewing is to establish the true desire and intent of the client to achieve health and balance through natural means. You must ascertain the depth and breadth of the client's faith to heal the self. To do this you will need an understanding of the client's spiritual philosophy.

The interview is also to build a platform for communications. If communication is honest and clear, then a bond of trust is built. A relationship based on truthful communications is essential to the success of the client reaching her goal of wellness.

The most important component that will always provide you with a clearer understanding is the knowledge and wisdom gained from actual one-on-one experience. This is only gained by practice.

To begin reaching this status of knowledge the following points are suggested:

- Learn to listen to your inner feelings and gain from your inner guidance. Most certainly you will allow your rational observation to be a guidepost and you will sincerely want to believe the statements of the client. Listen closely. How does it feel in your heart and other parts of your body? If you feel discomfort within yourself or from the client, then ask additional questions until you are completely satisfied.
- Establish your ground rules and be consistent.
- Establish a Practitioner's objective to attract clients in need of your healing ability. Clients are sent by God to create your continued growth, by confronting your focus in natural healing.
- It is helpful to write down your attributes and accomplishments and compare them with your healing objectives. Then you will have a benchmark for comparing your intent, direction of study and achievements in reaching these goals as a Practitioner.
- Open up to your innate potential and you will learn to assist your clients to confront their challenges. They will have effective healings and you will expand your working knowledge as a Practitioner.

Whatever your education or opinion of your spiritual development, know that you continue learning from all levels of discernment. The Practitioner must always discern if a decision is directed by her ego or her Higher Self's wisdom. If there is any thinking or wording using "I know" or "I will" or the likes thereof, take a more objective look at the origin of the motive, and for whom the action is to benefit. Ego is too often cloaked in the garments of "good intentions" and thinking that you know what is best for the client. The client is the healer and only the client knows her soul level of truth. You, the Practitioner, if faithful to your pledge, will strive humbly to be a selfless facilitator allowing God and the client to guide the client to the client's true needs. In this result you will share the reward of the client's healing through gaining new awareness and perceptual changes needed to correct the behavioral pattern and heal the emotional wound.

Remember, it is not the responsibility of the healer to accept all persons as clients. By interviewing the client you will have an understanding of the individual. Your acceptance is a commitment to the individual and to yourself. The Practitioner decides whether to accept or not accept the person being interviewed. If you do accept the client be sure to have them read and sign the Healing Agreement you design for your practice. To learn more about interviewing the client we refer you to the Home Study class *Esoteric Psychology and Anatomy.* These two classes comprise approximately eighteen lecture hours of information and group discussion.

The Interview

Review the Interview Questionnaire and clarify each person's questions. Explore the client's sincerity, desire and motivation to create an honest and nonresistant relationship with herself. Discuss the rapport necessary between the client and Practitioner to foster a truthful and honest relationship.

Have the client sign a Healing Agreement, because the client's commitment and full participation is important. We have found that a minimum of seven sessions is needed to fathom the depth of the client's challenges. The client may become asymptomatic prior to completing the seven sessions, but this does not mean the causal factor has been revealed and forgiven.

Explain the *Twenty-One Day Healing Cycle* and how after three sessions, the client will be clearing on all three levels of the heart. See the *Twenty-One Day Healing Cycle* explanation in Chapter Eight.

When you have determined from the interview that all conditions are favorable for positive intervention, you are in the position to accept the person as a client. This is a two-way street. Each must be willing to give freely and without resistance for the goals of wellness to be achieved. With this accomplished, your next step is to select the healing procedure that will facilitate this objective. These can be standard hands-on, full-body treatments, or affirmations.

Interviewing a Couple

It is suggested that when a spouse or loved one accompanies the potential client to the interview, interview the client first without the loved one present. Then invite the spouse or friend to join you. If this person presents conflicting input or contradiction about the client's habits and how the loved one is conscientious to do "just the right things", then red flag the case; know that the spouse or friend will most certainly inhibit or attempt to undermine the healing. Investigate the possible motives of both individuals. (Please refer to the section *Could the Beloved be Retarding the Healing*?)

Learning to Listen

As a Practitioner it is your responsibility to listen carefully to the phrases and words of the client. Reconstruct these words and thought-forms so that they provide new, positive and constructive key words. In this manner you provide additional support to the healing process.

The phrases below are only a few that you may hear from the client. What you are listening to is the negative and not the positive voice of the person. It is important that the individual regains faith in herself and in God. This is a parallel process, and must be undertaken step-by-step. Your role as a Practitioner is to offer assistance for the client to achieve her desired state of well-being. Help the client create positive affirmations from the experiences gained from recognizing old patterns and habits. Each client will have unique examples.

Old (ego)	**New** (unlimited in consciousness)
I cannot	I do not desire to…
I have a problem	I thank you for the challenge...
I am angry	I now communicate hurt feelings…
I do not trust my worth	I accept God's unlimited blessings...
I am not worthy of love	I know God loves me unconditionally ...
I have no choice	I always have freewill to choose again…

Additional reading: *Power Through Constructive Thinking*, The Power of Awareness, Neville (DeVorss) and *Sermon on the Mount* by Dr. Emmet Fox (Harper & Row). Additional study: *Intuitive Evaluation of Client Consciousness* (RPI Home Study Seminar)

Chapter 4

The Treatment

Treatment Selection Checklist

Before the beginning of the initial healing session, be sure that the following conditions have been met:

1. Client Interview Form filled out and placed in the client's file.
2. You have jointly established the client's goals.
3. The appropriate Healing Agreement has been signed, and a copy given to the client and a copy placed in his file.
4. You have established ground rules you feel are needed for the client. Remember, changes may need implementing once the healing begins.

Treatment Selection

Use the Full Body Treatment if the client has not accepted his freewill role of creating the challenges currently facing him or he has only a physical imbalance due to an accidental injury or physical exertion. An overload of stress is physical with an emotional charge. Stress is a result of an overloaded sympathetic nervous system (third chakra) where the ego has willed the body into imbalance

Use the Mental-Emotional Affirmation Treatment if the client has verbally stated his acceptance of his freewill role in creating the challenge. The sympathetic nervous system (ego) is now ready to allow the parasympathetic nervous system (fifth chakra) the opportunity to establish balance through the "rest and digest" mode of functioning.

Practitioner's and Client's Preparation

First prepare yourself mentally and emotionally for the healing. You must let go of the part that you will play in the healing. This aligns the conscious brain with the higher mind. In this state of "mindlessness" you prepare your mind to be open, allowing God's healing energy to flow through you without your ego's attachment. You must always remember that the client is the healer.

Prayer is always appropriate. Whether you choose a silent or verbal prayer to invite the protection of God to surround you and the client and to guide you during this healing is a personal choice. In our prayer, we ask for the presence of the Master Healer Jesus and ask that he place his hands over ours to guide the healing.

It is not uncommon to have the client request that we pray together. This is a special bond that you are creating. You experience the client directing his conscious mind to be open to the healing power of God. In so many healing challenges that we have witnessed, the client's faith has been the momentum and force to sustain the fragile body, and otherwise weak ego, to achieve a complete healing of the body and emotions.

The Physical Level Full Body Reiki Treatment

Hand Placement for the Healing

All healing sessions begin with the client in the supine (face up) position. Your hands are in Position #1: hands over the face. This provides you and the client the opportunity to center and open up to the energy. In this position you stimulate the sixth chakra and the pituitary gland. You are also balancing the upper respiratory sinus and nasal tissue and the eyes.

If you are not as knowledgeable about the anatomy covered by each hand position used in Reiki, we suggest that you review Chapter Seven of *Reiki Plus Natural Healing*, Fourth Edition. You will also find various books available to teach you human anatomy and about the systems of the body. A Practitioner should be knowledgeable of human anatomy and physiology.

To Implement the Energy

Once the client is comfortable on the healing table, with a pillow or bolster under his knees, a cover for warmth and the prayer complete, begin by placing your hands on the face in Position #1. It is time now to focus within and invoke the Second Degree energy of Reiki. When the face is balanced, proceed to Position #2. You are balancing the Crown Chakra and the pineal gland, the hypothalamus gland and the left and right hemispheres of the brain. Then proceed to Position #3 to treat the back of the head. Then continue to treat the torso front and back. One of the many reminders taught in First Degree when treating our client is that we do not touch the sexual or private parts of the body.

Clients with any respiratory disorder whose lungs have become congested with mucus are not to be treated in the prone position (face down, lying on the front of the torso). If a large amount of mucus is present in the lungs, a client in the face down position can experience restriction in his ability to breathe. This can result in an inadequate uptake of oxygen. Drowning or suffocation has resulted by placing persons in this position by persons untrained in proper medical procedures.

Remember to Reiki the client's legs and arms on the first treatment to assure that they have not overlooked any preexisting condition or old injury suffered by the limbs.

Allow the client time after the session to relax on the table quietly for integration of the healing work. It might be appropriate to discuss the dynamics of the healing during this integration time. Always ask the client if they wish to talk or be given space to assimilate the results of the healing.

Chapter 5

The Mental-Emotional Healing Symbol

Opening the Etheric Bodies

The Mental-Emotional Healing Symbol directly expands all eight Etheric Bodies more than basic Second Degree energy. This places the client in an open and vulnerable energy status. Clients are to be placed in the Mental-Emotional Healing Symbol only in a protective environment.

Do not administer healing under conditions that are subject to disharmonious energy influences. This may be when the healer or client is in an imbalanced emotional state, when there are animals or children playing or other disturbing noises invading the healing room. If you have to discontinue prior to completing the healing, close the client's energy bodies by placing your hands in Head Position #2 or the Closing Position where the thumbs touch the crown center and the tip of the middle fingers touch the top of the mastoid bone. This position immediately contracts the Etheric Bodies to a protective state controllable by the client.

A protective state means the client will be less vulnerable to environmental stimuli than she would be normally. Since each person has her own natural state of sensitivity, awareness of the client's degree of sensitivity is important. A person's sensitivity directly affects her ability to integrate insights presented during the healing.

Observe your client's posture, body language, verbal responses and eye contact or lack thereof. There are various opinions as to the meanings of these traits. Further study will enhance your perception. Ask questions and observe the verbal and nonverbal responses and body language that follow. The response gives you a personalized understanding of the client. General opinions always need tailoring, otherwise error lies in typecasting purely by external observation.

The Practitioner needs to evaluate the sensitivity of the client before each session. Explore the trials and confrontations that have challenged the client in the past. How has she dealt with them? Her response can range from total debilitation of her psyche to physical control of her fear nature. Control and composure express the differences between different psyches. Control is a third chakra function. Composure is the client's belief (fifth chakra) speaking the insight (sixth chakra) of her faith (seventh chakra) and trust (eighth chakra) in you.

A Hidden Karmic Danger!

With the Mental-Emotional Healing Symbol, you have the capacity to open the person's soul memory through the doorway of her unconscious mind. This is the potential of this symbol's energy, and infers another potential: its misuse. Since the mind is opened and can be communicated with telepathically by the Practitioner, clarity and intent are paramount. Healing is governed by God's will and the will of the client, not your own. This warrants restating: "Thy Will Be Done, Not Mine."

If an individual uses the telepathic powers of this symbol's energy to control the mind of the client, she is creating a great debt that will yield immediate return. Mind control means any suggestion verbal or nonverbal that is deceptive in nature, intending to usurp a person's freewill or forcing your "will" upon an individual (be it subtle and manipulative, or forceful). Therefore, never misuse the power of sacred energy. All energy from God is pure. It is unqualified energy until the nature of the person channeling the energy creates her design through intent. Please accept this advice. Always ask your Higher Self to guide all healing sessions. Remember that the ego is a strange being and will do its best to deceive the brain that "it, the ego" is not directing the healing process of the Practitioner's client; especially when this is a lesson chosen by the ego this lifetime to be learned. The ego also knows just what to say to the conscious mind in order to justify and rationalize the basis of discernment used, if the ego does not yet wish to surrender to divine guidance.

The Mental-Emotional Affirmation Treatment

To Attune for the Affirmation

Follow all of the steps for preparation covered in the Physical Body Treatment Procedure. Treat the Head Positions #1 and then Position #2. After these positions are balanced, you are ready to begin the Affirmation Treatment.

The Affirmation Position uses a special hand position for the Mental-Emotional Healing Symbol of Second Degree. You place your right hand on the Crown Chakra with the fingers pointing towards the forehead. Placing your hand in this manner puts your fingers in line with the body meridians. You may place your left hand either under the head or on the left side of the head. Takata taught her teachers to place the right hand across the crown with fingers pointing towards the left ear of the client, which crosses the meridians. It is our experience that the energy does not flow as well, and it often feels uncomfortable to the client. It has been known to even create pain in the head.

Visualize the Mental-Emotional Healing Symbol being written with the mind's eye in purple light on the back of the right hand, and then nonverbally intone the words three times in your mind's voice. Then visualize the Empowerment Symbol being drawn in golden-white light directly on top of the Mental-Emotional Healing Symbol. Continue by nonverbally intoning the words three times. Before we proceed with any verbal affirmation, we must allow the client to reach a receptive state of consciousness.

How long does it take to make the energy bond? This bond is an energetic synchronization between you and the client. What develops is a symbiotic blending of your energy field with the energy field of the client. You must learn to know this feeling of when it is time. If you have experience with operating automotive, airplane or marine engines, you have heard and felt when the engine was at an rpm that was just right. The engine begins to resonate what is often called a harmonic overtone. It sounds and feels good and in harmony with itself. The symbiotic blending of two energy fields has a similar feeling but inaudible sound, unless you are clairaudient. The time to reach this blending might be three to five minutes after placing the symbols on the Crown Chakra.

Once the energy bond is clearly established you can begin the verbal interaction with the client. Be sure that you offer only positive suggestions to the client, if needed, to help the client regain or realign her mental and emotional focus. If the client has shared her affirmation with you before the healing, you may choose to speak the affirmation gently and clearly at this point as a reminder.

Then the client speaks the affirmations. It is the choice of the client whether she chooses to do so out loud or silently. Either way establishes the client's role as the healer, as she must implement the affirmations to begin changing her mental and emotional attitude. An affirmation does not eradicate the lessons of life; it simply helps the client to focus on the positive side of the opportunities she has chosen to learn.

Allow the client to remain in this opened and altered state of consciousness long enough to emotionally and mentally register the affirmation she has co-created with God and with her Higher Self. An affirmation establishes a new trust in the mind of the client, which must be nurtured by proactive participation of the mind, body and emotions in aligned desire to allow Spirit the opportunity to manifest the changes in all of the client's chakras.

Now close down the Mental-Emotional energy by placing your hands in Position #2 on the head. Remain in this position for 30 seconds to one minute, before moving to the next position on the body. Complete the Reiki treatment by balancing all standard positions and needed specific imbalance positions for the client. Treating with Second Degree is no different than First Degree in regard to attaining a state of balance for each position, although it may take less time using Second or Third Degree Reiki energy. Remember that you can increase the healing energy given to a deficient area of the body by doing multiple Second Degree Empowerments on your hands.

Could the Beloved be Retarding the Healing?

A client who seems inconsistent in her psycho-physical healing curve may be continuing a victim role. Did the client come to you on the insistence of the beloved in her life? Did the client appear in your office with her spouse? Did they contradict each other's answers? Were any questions raised in your mind when listening to this scenario or did you just let the questions pass by? Was the potential client submissive to her spouse? Was it difficult to get an answer from the potential client without the spouse answering?

These are just a few of the possible indicators that you have a potential client who is not going to be a sincere client. More likely, someone who behaves in this manner will become inconsistent once you have accepted her as a client. History has proven that the client who is not self-motivated is not interested in achieving a complete healing. She endures the healing sessions to please her beloved. Her interest is not in achieving wellness, but in continuing her game of victim.

This game is not uncommon. Oftentimes the victim or helpless role is played to allow the spouse or friend to feel a sense of being needed by the client. The participants can have any possible physical/emotional relationship. If the client begins to show signs of becoming well and the partner senses his "need position" being eliminated, he may begin to undermine the healing process. It often accounts for the incomplete healing, even after the client has progressed towards wellness.

The motivation for keeping the loved one sick or emotionally helpless may stem from the spouse's neediness. The spouse may be playing the role as an enabler in a codependent relationship. This is a classic case of conditional love, where the spouse, who expressed a desire to see the loved one well, may truly be frightened of no longer being needed. He may sense that his position of importance is no longer important in the same manner as before. If he is no longer needed to care for his spouse, then his role will change, and change, as we know, can stimulate fear. This fear manifests as resistance, and individuals are naturally resistant to change, even though the world is in constant change.

If you are presented with this situation, you will have to confront both your client and the enabling codependent partner, if the healing work is to progress on a positive note. Otherwise, to continue to work only one side of the fence leaves the other unresolved. In this situation it may be advisable to refer your client and the partner to a holistic and spiritually minded licensed counselor, psychologist, or if needed, a psychiatrist.

When the Client Undermines the Healing

We cannot say that all inconsistencies or incomplete healing patterns is the undermining by another person. The patterns can simply be the act of the client realizing that she is not ready to face her challenges. Too great of a challenge can come from many factors. Each case in healing is unique. It can be that you, the Practitioner, have misread the signals from the client and pushed too hard too quickly. This is not uncommon.

The client indicates the desire to achieve wellness and you have the zeal to urge him onward. You may be saying that all things are in divine time, so how can it be too much healing? It can be. Divine time is always in accord with real time. We can get overanxious and jump too far, too soon, before all that has been revealed to the client in the healings is assimilated by the client. If this occurs and it is recognized quickly, you will normally retain your client. If not caught soon enough, you will lose a client who will find other pressing matters to attend to and cannot keep her appointments.

If the client begins to miss appointments, we suggest that you review with the client her resistance to continue with the healing sessions. Pinpoint and discuss the challenges that are pushing the person too hard. Let the client know that she can put these challenges on the back burner. This allows time for less stressful memories to be processed, laying a firmer foundation upon which to build.

Should the healing procedure be changed? Yes. You might also need to approach the healing from the physical level only, to treat the client's full body with Second or Third Degree energy. If this standard approach evidences an increase in physical well-being, improved health and attitude, you are facilitating a healing. The proof is whether the person maintains the physical healing after the completion of the healing sessions. If so, and if other sub-matrix and chakra-related psycho-physical disorders do not pop up in its place, then you can measure the healing a success.

Congenital Disorders

Congenital disorders, whether they are physical or emotional, present the Practitioner with a different set of circumstances to work with. The goal of healing for congenital disorders is to understand the chosen lessons and to have a positive attitude under the circumstances.

A complete physical or neurological healing might be an unrealistic goal for the client. The desire may be present and yet the mind or body is to remain unchanged. When the client sees the challenges and begins to understand and accept the conditions chosen by her prior to birth, the healing is complete. They then begin living in a co-creative relationship with themselves and God. Their mission is to co-exist in a positive attitude and fulfill their destiny chosen for this lifetime from a positive consciousness.

The Healing Process

The Treatment procedure of Reiki as passed down by Mrs. Takata is to treat physical imbalances three days in a row. This is still true whether you are a First, Second or Third Degree Practitioner and treating purely physical body imbalances. Treatments will then be spaced apart over several days to allow the body its ability to regain its healing ability. Then you objectively wish to have clients move to weekly treatments. Once they are stable and the body is regaining strength, you can space the sessions two weeks apart. It will of course reach a point where they will not require treatments, unless the clients do not regain the function of their immune system or emotional center.

Once a client has achieved the desired goal of wellness, she may ask for maintenance treatments. Weekly or biweekly treatments support the client's immune system from stress. Continued treatments allow the person to give herself the gift of love. It continues the client's development of self-worth and self-approval to receive unconditional love

Also remember that if a client requires additional healing during your care, you may remind her that you can treat with Absentia, rather than a personal hands-on session. The value of this treatment is no less than the value of a treatment in person, especially if your client is in a restive posture during the time you will send the treatment. We see many clients in this manner due to their physical residence being hundred or thousands of miles from us. This is a wonderful means to expand your practice and provide excellent healing assistance to the client.

It is important for the Practitioner to have a working knowledge of the material presented in Chapter Eleven, Specific Imbalances. This material is further developed in the elective Home Study course *Esoteric Anatomy*, where the Practitioner learns how to develop an esoteric thinking perspective and combine the results of enhanced intuitive processes with known treatment procedures for an imbalance. When treating the causal factor on the unconscious level, the client will need appropriate treatment for physical imbalances as well. Never lose sight of the need to treat the whole person physically and emotionally. The therapeutic approach of *Reiki Plus* concerns the healing of the mind, body and emotions. Since the approach deals with the whole person, the application contained in this section requires the direct participation of the client to affect the process of the healing.

When the awareness of the client is opened into her unconscious mind, she gains knowledge either previously unknown, unseen and/or unassociated to the specific characteristics of her psycho-physical imbalance. This awareness precipitates the healing confrontation that follows, for now she is armed with awareness and has the choice to use freewill from this time forward. The healing crisis is not purely the process of moving from chronic, to sub-acute and then to acute levels; it is now compounded with the reality of the person involved and the necessity that she must also be confronted to cleanse the slate for the healing process to continue. The act of self-forgiveness must be initiated. When the client can forgive self and be open to divine love, she can then forgive those whom she once considered to be her victimizers. Forgiveness is presented in Chapter Seven of this book.

Chapter 6

The *Psycho-Therapeutic Reiki Plus* Concept

Psycho-Therapeutic Reiki Plus addresses healing at the soul level. The process of this advanced training teaches the Practitioner how to safely and effectively work with the four levels of memory.

Each level of memory has an interconnected compound-complex matrix of stimuli woven in the chakra bodies (Etheric Bodies) surrounding the physical body. Negative and painful memories clog the lines of communication between the physical body and the chakra bodies. Unresolved or misunderstood pain and emotional trauma overload and breakdown the etheric body's communications, the neural network linking these chakra bodies to the body's internal systems.

Pain occurs from actions that resulted in perceived disapproval from self or someone important to the person. If this pattern persists, then the ego is altered in a manner that will eventually create imbalance in a body part or body system. The imbalanced pattern creates a superimposed tapestry over the soul imprint. The result of this new tapestry is the loss of access to the individual's higher consciousness where knowledge and wisdom are innately stored. The higher consciousness is the ego's link to the soul's lessons, and spiritual perception and insight.

The strength and thrust of the *Psycho-Therapeutic Reiki Plus* healing technique is the gentle and safe unweaving of the superimposed tapestry of painful choices. Once this begins, the reweaving of new soul aligned patterns that build a renewed desire to choose healthy opportunities are set in motion. The objective of soul level healing is to rebuild personal desire and motivation to choose healthy, fun and joyful opportunities. To assist this rebuilding of the ego-soul connection, the client begins to create a strong supporting foundation by understanding the laws of spiritual discernment. Discernment avails itself to activate transmutation through the laws of forgiveness.

The Practitioner trained in *Psycho-Therapeutic Reiki Plus* is taught to facilitate the client's healing by helping the client to establish a clear perspective for viewing the "old" pattern, and how to integrate the new insight gained from each session. The result is clear recognition of similar stimuli when such stimulus confronts the client after the healing. This teaches the client how to lessen or eliminate the need to repeat old patterns.

The pattern that has been woven from the seed to fertilization will often be extremely complex. The pattern exists within her conscious, subconscious and unconscious mind on various levels at the same time.

Uncovering the multi-faceted connections to the existing imbalance is achieved by the healing. This technique helps the individual to become aware of all the acts and omissions during the past that have compounded the growth of the unknown imbalance.

The challenges facing the client are gently integrated by the *Psycho-Therapeutic Reiki Plus* technique. The historical events stored within the body provide revelations and positive directions to implement change. The steps for integrating change are unique to the specific circumstances.

The client's awareness of her old thinking and behavioral patterns is needed to initiate changes when faced with old stimuli. This is followed by active utilization of the new insight gained from each healing session. The client's continued recognition provides the next step for positive change, which is eliminating the instinct to react from the third chakra, which is a fear based response. When the client no longer reacts from fear, she then allows her life to be directed by the truth of God's unconditional love.

The Compound-Complex Matrix

There are four natures of memory that form an individual's complex memory system. All four levels of memory can be found lodged in an associated chakra center, body part, organ or gland (re: *Esoteric Anatomy*). We call this general classification of memory somatic tissue memory. There is often sensitivity or pain when this area or point on the body is touched or palpated by the client.

- Associated conscious memory—where a person acknowledges freewill choice. The client is consciously aware of the connections between her current actions and past traumas.

- Unassociated conscious memory—everyday behaviors that stimulate the pattern of imbalance automatically. The client is unaware that current conflicts and confrontations with others are related to past traumas. The logical ego mind will insist that the current situation has nothing to do with past traumas or patterns. This is where the client may project anger, sadness, rejection, abandonment, etc, onto other people in her life, and possibly even onto her spiritual teachers, or you as the facilitator, rather than taking responsibility for her part in the lesson. Her free-will choice in inviting the person to participate in her life must be acknowledged and forgiven, before the confrontational pattern will cease to present itself to her over and over again.

- Subconscious memory— The subconscious is a composite of complex combinations of psycho-physical impressions, reactions (conscious or unconscious), fears, etc., that are stored in the unconscious memory bank. The subconscious mind is always awake and every experience of our lives sends programming messages to the subconscious mind.

- Collective unconscious memory—this is an accumulative memory carried by the soul from ego to ego, and life to life. Unconscious memories carry the stimuli of soul choice that then designs the script potential for soul evolution. In other words, this level of memory sets the stage for the lessons a person has the opportunity to learn in this lifetime. Again, freewill choice is instrumental. However, its potential to stimulate expanded consciousness is dependent upon the discretion and discerning ability of the ego. The soul memory is simply our connection to all of the past knowledge stored within our mind. This begins with our individual soul's birth from the Universal Mind.

It is from the soul's storage bank that all choices are made for each incarnation. Each soul chooses the lessons needed to complete this segment of the soul's growth. These choices include a mission or purpose for the ego and its personality to grow to fulfillment, the parents needed as proper models, the necessary socioeconomic, religious philosophical, familial and genetic conditions necessary to stimulate the ego's journey in this lifetime.

An individual's choices determine the path and its portended lessons at any and every given moment of life. Let's explore how freewill choices, when used without awareness or discretion, develop the compound complex matrix resulting in painful lessons.

The birth of a tree begins with the planting of a seed. Our challenges in life parallel the same metamorphic process, in a pattern with seemingly no logic. Once the seed of a behavior pattern is planted and begins to mature, it will follow a unique course leading to the challenges now present in the client's life. A very alarming fact is that the seed has continued to germinate new plants from the original seedling. This is really the process of compounding an original trauma into similar, yet apparently unrelated, incidents of life. Not only has the client planted new processes from existing behavioral patterns and characteristics, she has oftentimes compounded them by the intertwining of the root system. When this occurs, the new seedling is an offshoot of a pre-existing psycho-physical behavioral pattern. These patterns can be difficult for the client to identify.

There are infinite points of origin from which the unrecognized imbalances manifest in the body, mind, emotions and spirit of an individual. Once the individual begins an imbalanced psycho-physical behavioral pattern and becomes comfortable with or accepting of this pattern, it becomes increasingly difficult to recognize the disruptive aspects of the pattern. Not until the psycho-physical pattern becomes a physiological or psychological dysfunction or disease is the individual possibly willing to consider that something is amiss in her regime. If she chooses to totally heal a pattern, first she must realize her participation in choosing to create the lesson. The lack of personal responsibility and the indiscretion of free will are key elements that must be acknowledged by the client before permanent healing can begin to take place.

Transmutation

The *Psycho-Therapeutic Reiki Plus* technique is used to open the door to the unconscious and subconscious memory fields of the client, which is the door to the ego, the mind and the soul. Insight gained from the healing technique reveals the client's imbalanced emotional patterns. She learns that each pattern has deeper layers of intertwined nature. These associated layers, form the compound-complex matrix. These layers can be understood only to the degree the client personally experiences the power and healing of forgiveness, which rebuilds her faith and is the gateway to learning to trust herself.

New associations will be discovered since they are normally safely buried below the surface of awareness, entwined in obscure networks of dysfunctional patterns of behavior that await unraveling. Again, we see the opportunity for the client to delve deeper into the associations, releasing her from her own entrapment. When the layers of association are brought to the surface of awareness, the client can begin to expand beyond previously accepted protective mechanisms keeping her safe in her own world. If the client is willing to accept the necessary changes, she will continue her healing process.

To be effective we must understand the complex process of transmutation. The transmutation of a thought, a craving, a desire, a behavior pattern or especially an unrecognized or unknown behavior, allows the individual to transform her opinion and let go of the attachment to the past pattern. This is true even when the conscious mind remembers the act as pleasurable at the same time it inflicted emotional or physical discomfort. Transmutation is the process of the client becoming consciously aware of her freewill choices so that she can then release herself from her attachment to her behavioral pattern through forgiveness. The following steps outline the basic concept:

1. To transmute associated conscious, unassociated conscious, subconscious or collective unconscious memories, the trauma and/or origins of the psycho-physical, psycho-emotional or psycho-mental

disorders, the client needs to be aware that a behavioral pattern within the complex ego-personality is imbalanced.

2. To accomplish modification, it is beneficial for the client to understand that her indiscretion and freewill choice created her current pattern of behavior. This challenge can either be a carryover from the soul memory or newly created in this incarnation.

3. The individual's recognition and acceptance of the stimulus triggering her imbalanced reaction allows her to change the pattern of behavior.

4. The client is then able to bless the chosen experience, the personal and joint relationship(s) of the challenge, and to release her attachment to the pattern.

5. The client needs to forgive herself for all her considered wrong actions. This is not condoning moral wrongdoing nor supporting irresponsibility. All experiences in life are for learning to bond with the true God Self. God forgives. Humankind has the challenge to learn forgiveness, trust and faith. Our life experiences are best understood when seen as learning experiences, not as errors, mistakes or sins.

Transmutation effects change. The individual who never consciously associated her pattern of thought, action and reaction with the psycho-physical imbalance may be reluctant to admit a need for change. We often have become comfortable with the behavioral characteristics developed over many years. Behavioral patterns are released when the client understands the lesson through experience, confrontation and forgiveness. An individual's demonstration of her intense desire, faith and commitment to heal is often rewarded through the power of grace by God, whereby healing is bestowed. When the individual is blessed by grace, the experience may be integrated and healed without having completely conscious recognition of how all of the pieces fit together. The synergy of Spirit integrates the conscious and unconscious components of the soul through the heart. After the healing occurs, insight may unfold that allows the full lesson to be revealed and understood.

The *Psycho-Therapeutic Reiki Plus* Technique

The *Psycho-Therapeutic Reiki Plus* technique makes it easier for the individual to recognize these attachments: the threads of the compound-complex matrix are revealed through the weekly healings.

The essential key to the healing is to gently reveal past traumas and memories so that the client can perceive confrontational patterns in a new way. This new way of perceiving is the benchmark of the transmutation process. The client gently experiences the causal factor and all of the unknown layers of the imbalance or psycho-emotional pattern from its seed origin. The psyche, in a healing mode, sends positive messages to the chakra centers and chakra bodies, allowing the physical body to regain balance. Thus, the client experiences a re-patterning of her total personality: its opinions, judgments, attitudes, anger and other seemingly automatic functions. Essentially, this translates to mean that the client learns to have greater self-control, and experiences greater clarity and insight into her challenges, both physically and emotionally.

Where the client once may have blamed another person for her problems prior to experiencing the transmutation process, she is now able to see her freewill choice in the pattern and acknowledge her soul's lesson. She is able to forgive herself for her choices, thereby letting go of holding another person responsible for her pain. This allows her to free up a tremendous amount of emotional energy. She will also begin to watch painful patterns fall away.

The power of forgiveness is an essential part of this healing technique and is covered in depth in Chapter Seven.

The Practitioner trained in this technique is taught to facilitate the client's healing by helping the client to establish a clear perspective for viewing the old pattern, and learning how to integrate the new insight gained from each session. The result is clear recognition of similar stimuli when such stimuli confront the client after the healing. This teaches the client how to lessen or eliminate the need to repeat negative response patterns.

Chapter 7

Forgiveness

Forgiveness is the key to complete healing. Each memory a person judges as an error holds her in the stagnation of sin and guilt, and it is for these actions of perceived error that forgiveness must be accepted and given. In Chapter One, from the Lord's Prayer meditation, we learned that the third chakra corresponds to the forgiveness of self, for the misuse of our will. Life is the process of learning how to choose the thoughts and actions that allow our heart to be at peace with God. This can only be a reality if the choices nurture our Godself with inner peace. Otherwise, choices made may not be our personal truth. Such choices may be made to make another person happy or to live another person's value system. Under these circumstances an individual gives up her freewill to live in a state of unhappiness or even sickness. It is from this state of perception that a person limits her sight.

Let us share a little insight with you about the shadow clients can cast upon their lives: they are walking backwards into the future with tunnel vision. Their hands are locked around the handles of a wheelbarrow, loaded with all of the wrongs of the past. They only have to let go of the handles to detach from the past. They no longer need to wonder why the tunnel has appeared to be so dark, for now with their hands free, they can turn around and be embraced by the Light.

Awareness about all of their past choices presents them the opportunity to take a committed posture of insuring that the future is not the same as the past. Many people have a tendency to be a bit too hard on themselves. However, since this is a freewill choice, it will only bring the awareness sooner or later that seeing in the Light also allows the healing to be a gentle procedure. For as clients embrace the act of surrendering to their Godself, their egos' struggle to direct their will from the emotional leverage point begins to dissolve. Each experience of surrendering allows their faith to build a firm foundation for their developing belief system.

They learn in that very moment what the statement "Let go, Let God" really means. These will no longer be incomprehensible words. These words will be a new foundation for a spiritual reality and the platform from which self-forgiveness, and the forgiveness of those whom they consider injured them, and the thanking of that person, can completely release them from the quagmire of their old illusions of reality. They can build the new tomorrow, today. Forgiveness allows a person to learn how to walk one footstep at a time. This is a path to healing the personality's separation from the soul and awakening to the reality of Spirit.

A Procedure for Forgiveness

Forgiveness is the act of opening one's heart to the full relationship with the people and patterns that have been the catalysts for closing oneself off from a part of life. The forgiveness process takes us through five major steps. For the sake of example we will consider the catalyst for choosing to close down one's heart has been another person.

Golden-pink light represents the divine love and wisdom always radiating from God upon the earth to all creation. The daily cycle of sunrise and sunset is a bathing of this golden-pink light from the horizon upon the earth. We begin to transform on etheric and cellular levels when we, as individualized ego-conscious humans, make a conscious decision to participate in accepting God's healing. God has patiently awaited for us to let go of our self-deceived and arrogant ego and breathe in unconditional divine love. We begin to co-create a physical/spiritual receptor that aligns the physical body to receive the harmony manifesting in the subtle bodies, our chakras. We are humbled because we stop fighting to control the fear of unworthiness, and in humility can begin to experience emotionally the cleansing by fire and release our own heart-crushing pain.

We take the first of the infinite number of steps directed by the spiritual principle, *Just for today I will accept my many blessings.* This breaks the old mold of unworthiness and opens the door to the light of God's own essence to enter our consciousness. We embrace the feeling that we are worthy to receive God's many and unlimited blessings.

In each of these steps of the Forgiveness Meditation, you breathe in God's golden-pink light into your heart. Then, from your heart breathe the golden-pink light into the heart of the other person until he is full of God's love and light. During any of these steps you may, in your mind, ask the other person for forgiveness for carrying the issue inside your heart for so long. You may also simply focus on your heart being open to the full relationship with the other without any words. Keep in mind, however, that words spoken from the heart can be very powerful and healing.

Also, do not confused being in a full relationship with another person as having to accept everything that the other person does, says and believes. We have the responsibility to choose the most loving choice in any situation. Many times this choice means we, in fact, do not accept the other's actions. For instance, it is quite natural to be fully available to another person, openly sharing our thoughts and feelings with him, and not be in full agreement with all his choices or actions. The anger we harbor towards another person churns within us and affects us, while keeping in focus those dynamics that we wish were not present.

Forgiving and opening your heart to a full relationship means that you express with clarity that which is in your heart. You acknowledge that the other has his own path and that you have your path. You recognize that God is within the soul of the other, and that you choose forgiveness for the higher good of all concerned, including yourself.

You begin the Forgiveness Meditation by allowing your heart to choose a theme or memory. To accomplish this, center yourself and breathe in through the top of your head, the Crown Chakra. Allow the golden-white light of the Cosmic Fire to fill the spine and then fill the body. You will soon breathe effortlessly and experience the rhythmic pulse of the dura membrane fluid flowing up and down the spine. Now you are ready to go into your heart and ask "What is the most important memory I need to forgive today?" Unconsciously, your heart will scan your body through the central nervous system's connection with the physical and chakra bodies. The memory for today and the related dynamics will be acknowledged and presented to you.

1. Take yourself to a warm sandy beach, where you sit awaiting the spectacular illumination of the sunrise. Then you today breathes God's golden-pink light into your heart from the sun cresting the ocean's horizon. Fill your heart with God's unconditional divine love and forgiveness, knowing that you are worthy to receive what God has patiently awaited for you to accept. You are surrendering your ego and accepting God's ever present forgiveness.

2. Once your heart is full of the golden-pink light, see you at the age of the memory sitting in front of you. Breathe from the heart of you today, God's golden-pink light into the heart of you at the age of the memory. Send forgiveness and unconditional love. Then enter the body of you at the age of the memory, and looking at you today from your eyes then, hear yourself speak the words of forgiveness to you today for having carried you at the age of the memory these many years, months, or days, not forgiven inside of your heart (and possibly an organ or in a system of the anatomy). Now thank yourself for the opportunity of this healing today.

3. Now merge you at the age of the memory and you today by opening your arms, hugging and opening the hearts of each self. Allow the two of you to become one. Then remain looking out through the eyes of both selves. You look out through the eyes of both selves because to forgive does not mean to forget the lesson our painful choices created. We learn from choices and hopefully do not repeat the same lesson.

4. When you have accomplished this merging, look out at the participant in the memory you have invited to teach you in this learning experience. This person may be your own self, at another time in your life, as it might be a pattern or habit repeating itself.

Breathe golden-pink light into the heart of this person. Ask him/her to forgive you for having carried him these many years, months, or days not forgiven inside of your heart (and possibly an organ or system of the anatomy). Now thank him for the opportunity of this healing today.

5. Now see this same person in the present moment of his life, whether he is alive or in spirit. Breathe from your heart into his heart and visualize his heart being filled with the golden-pink light. Forgive the person for his trespasses and ask him to forgive you for your trespasses.

When you forgive the person, this breaks the energy connection and begins the spiritual level of healing between the two of you. Thank the participant for the opportunity of this experience, for without it and the person's participation, you would never have known this was an issue restricting your spiritual and soul growth.

When you are able to offer the other the full blessings of God's unconditional love you will be ready to be fully open to the relationship. Further, once you have completed the forgiveness process you will also be able live with more acceptance of others' choices as you claim responsibility for your choices to an even fuller degree. The process of forgiveness is a self-empowering process. This process creates a more integrated connection with God's energy, and takes one from being a victim to seeing the situation as it looks from a spiritual perspective. Forgiveness facilitates our growth and healing, and allows us to gain a deeper spiritual understanding of our heavenly gift of freewill choice.

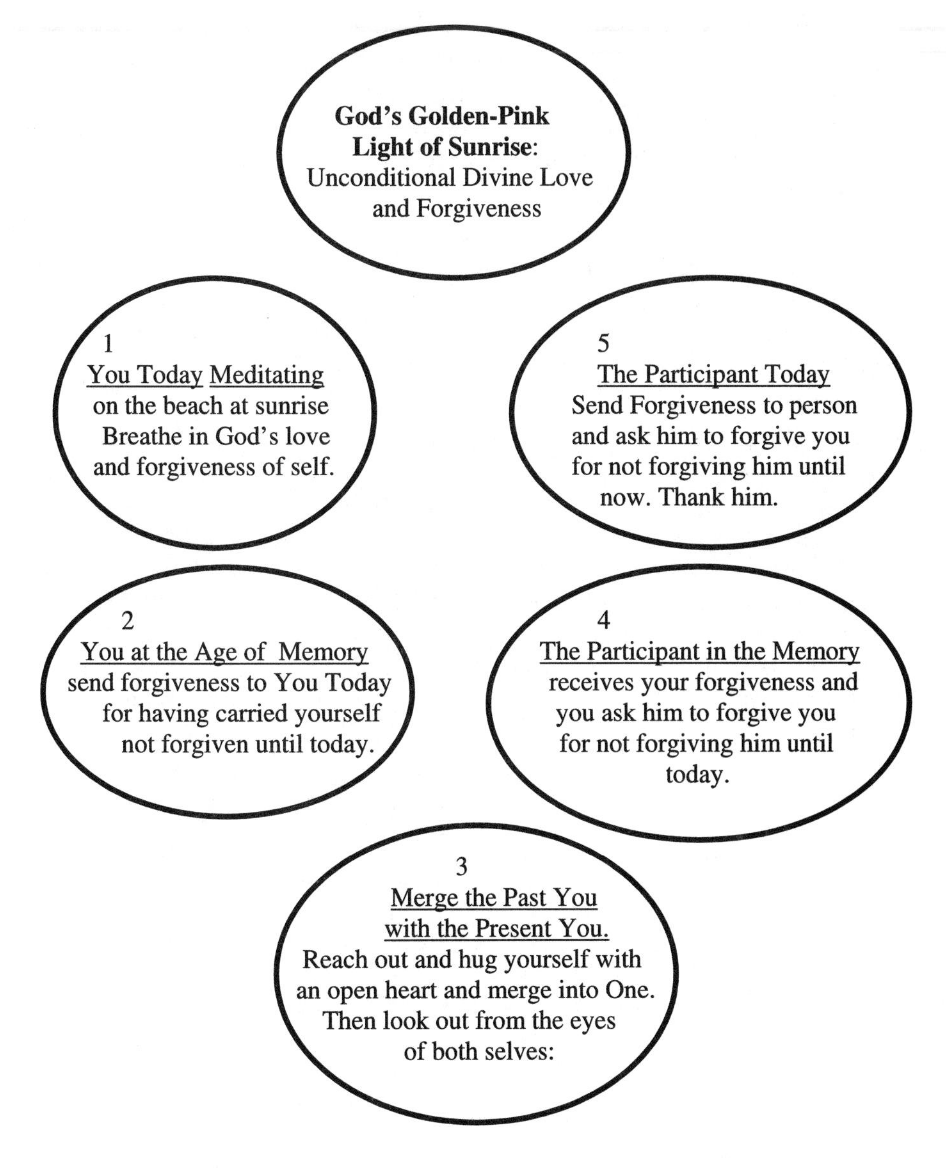

Through Forgiveness all Things are Possible

Chapter 8

The Twenty-One Day Healing Cycle

The Healing Curve

We know from experience that the quality of health a person first sets as her goal will be upgraded once the healing has begun. She will realize that there are many layers in the sub-matrix, and her perceptions of wellness take on new horizons. This process is due in part to the dynamics of the *Twenty-One Day Healing Cycle*.

When the client receives a healing, she begins a *Twenty-One Day Healing Cycle*. The twenty-one days is a time during which the client will have new insights and lessons presented to her, as related to the healing she received. In other words, whatever the client chooses to work on in the healing will stimulate things to be brought up out of her unconscious and subconscious, and out of her chakra bodies, so that the issues can be dealt with and healed. This process can be broken down into three week-long processes.

Week Number One

Week One begins on the day of the healing, and the client will spend twenty-four hours in the first chakra. The following day, she will cycle into the second chakra, and spend twenty-four hours there. The process continues day by day, chakra by chakra, until one week has passed. We call this the "I Week". It should be noted that the two heart chakras, the fourth (vital) heart, and the eighth (divine) heart, operate together on day four of the week-long process.

During this entire "I" week, the client is primarily operative from the third chakra, or the ego self. The lessons presented will usually be of the theme *"How I have willed my will"*. Issues of control, will power, misuse of power and control, feeling controlled by another person, awareness of having allowed an unhealthy pattern to continue, etc. are all possible themes that may surface during this first week. The client may be very angry all of a sudden. Confrontations can occur with family members, co-workers, or a boss. Usually there will be something about the behavior of this other person that relates to the theme of the client's healing, and therefore, the situation is arising to allow the client to see the pattern, and to forgive the choice of the pattern.

Chakra Centers

One Chakra per Day for Seven Days

This Cycle Occurs Three Times During the Twenty-One Days: One Cycle per week

1. **Day One**-First Chakra-Red: Survival, Instinct, Life force.
2. **Day Two**-Second Chakra-Orange: Sexuality and Creativity.
3. **Day Three**-Third Chakra-Yellow: Ego, Will, Control, Self-control and Creative Intellect.
4. **Day Four**-Fourth Chakra-Crystal: Heart where Light touches all Emotions and Feelings. The Eighth Chakra is also operative on Day Four and is Emerald Green.
5. **Day Five**-Fifth Chakra-Blue: Communication, Hearing, Listening, Speaking.
6. **Day Six**-Sixth Chakra-Purple: Perception, Left and Right Brain Balance.
7. **Day Seven**-Seventh Chakra-Golden-White: Illumination and Illusion.

First Week: How I have willed my will.
I - 3rd Chakra (the Adrenal Glands)

1. I acknowledge my instincts and expressions of energy.
2. I acknowledge my sexuality and any unexpressed creative needs
3. I acknowledge my will and ego conflict to be in control of others.
5. I acknowledge my emotions and need to have clear feelings.
6. I acknowledge my thoughts and hear the truth of my words.
7. I acknowledge my separation and division blocking clear sight.
8. I acknowledge my Light for I AM the potential of the Christ.

Week Number Two

Once Week One is completed, the client cycles back through the chakras again, beginning at the first chakra and continuing through the seventh chakra, again noting the fourth and eighth chakras operate together on day four of the week. We call this week the "Thy Week".

During this week of cycling back through the chakras, the client is primarily operative from the fourth chakra, and the theme is *"Surrendering my will to Thy will"*. This week offers the opportunity to see things from another perspective. Rather than operating from the ego, the client has the opportunity to surrender her will to "Thy will" so that she can learn a more positive way of dealing with challenges, conflicts, and frustrations. This is the true meaning and reality of the phrase "Let Go, Let God". Surrendering is a letting go of the ego's struggle, so that the client can open to receive new insight into how to approach a situation differently.

Themes and patterns from the first week may resurface, but the client may handle them differently during this week if she has adopted the posture of surrendering her ego, opening her heart, and accepting responsibility for her choices so that her soul can learn, forgive and move forward. If the client embraces this reality, true healing takes place. Upon finishing this week, the client will then enter the final week of the *Twenty-One Day Healing Cycle.*

Second Week: Surrendering My Will to Thy Will
THY - 4th Chakra (the Heart)

1. I accept Right Action by asking Thy direction.
2. I accept Thy creative flow to balance inner needs.
3. I accept Thy Will desiring to learn surrender.
4. I accept Thy Love which is harmonious and unconditional.
5. I accept Thy truths to clarify my beliefs so that I might hear you.
6. I accept Thy perception to clarify my division and vision.
7. I accept my Christ Self to Light my vision and way.

Week Number Three

The third week is known as the "Divine Week". Here, the theme is *"I trust the Divine within me,"* and the client is primarily operative from the eighth chakra, the higher, or divine heart. Once again, the cycle through the chakras occurs and patterns may again surface.

The opportunity of this week is for the client to find the "win-win" in the confrontational situations that may occur. Surrendering may come more quickly; clear perception of one's choices, lessons, and responsibility may come more quickly. Forgiveness occurs more effortlessly as the client experiences the freedom it brings. Insights are integrated and the client is able to stay centered in a more effective way. The client begins to operate from her Higher Self more frequently, rather than from her ego self, which has been the past pattern.

Third Week: I Trust the Divine Within Me
Divine – 8th Chakra (Thymus Gland)

1. I Am Divine Action and *trust the Divine within Me.*
2. I Am Divine Creativity and *trust the Divine within Me.*
3. I Am Divine Creative-Will and *trust the Divine within Me.*
4. I Am Divine Love feeling and *trusting the Divine within Me*
5. I Am Divine Expression of beliefs and *trust the Divine within me.*
6. I Am Divine perception and *trust the Divine within Me.*
7. I Am Divine Light and *trust the Divine within Me.*

Of course when the client is seen on a weekly basis, then each week begins a new *Twenty-One Day Healing Cycle.* Thus, the cycles overlap each other and help speed along the healing process. When forgiveness of self and others takes place, this is the quickest way for a client to move through her lessons so that life can become more joyful, free, and expressive.

It has also been found that a gap in sessions beyond fourteen days can be a setback. If this break in sessions occurs, go back to the last healing and review the case. Relapse is not uncommon, since several sessions were missed. A person can sustain crisis management and challenges more easily when sessions are weekly. Also, the influence of the twenty-eight-day lunar cycle can be observed: every seventh day the moon moves to square, to oppose, to square again, and then to conjunct the beginning moment of the first healing. The moon is the emotional center of the individual and therefore the seven-day cycles play another role in the dynamics of the healee's journey toward wellness.

When reflecting upon the *Twenty-One Day Healing Cycle*, be sure to consider the "I-Thy-Divine" (Chapter Nine) for balancing the psycho-physical, emotional and mental parts of the personality. In a manner of speaking, each healing session not only has the potential to balance the unresolved issues of the previous sessions, it also has the potential to open the door even wider for a healing on a deeper level during each subsequent session.

By the end of the third or fourth session the "average" imbalance will have made a turn upwards. From there, it will maintain a progressive incline toward wholeness, harmony, self-love, self-appreciation and joy. You will note a distinct difference in the client's attitude, voice modulation, facial expressions and auric field. The feeling you will experience is the warmth in your heart, knowing that you have been an instrument of God helping another soul return to harmony. This is truly the reward of the healing profession.

The "I – Thy – Divine" Layering and Unfolding

	Days:					
Treatment	**1-7**	**8–14**	**15–21**	**22–28**	**29–35**	**36–42**
One	I	Thy	Divine			
Two		I	Thy	Divine		
Three			I	Thy	Divine	
Four				I	Thy	Divine
Five					I	Thy
Six						I

Sequenced treatments on a seven-day basis provide wonderful insight and unfolding for the client. Note that by treatment three, the client begins to work on three layers of unfolding (I, Thy and Divine simultaneously) and continues to do so until the treatments are discontinued.

Chapter 9

I-Thy-Divine

There are three levels of the heart. Each level applies to our personal healing and evolutionary process in the expansion of our "bubble" of cosmic consciousness. We can correlate these three levels to the *Twenty-One Day Healing Cycle of Initiation* and the Healing Curve, which represent the balancing period after each level of Reiki initiation or the beginning of a healing process.

In this chapter we will address the progression of consciousness through the Rays of Initiation, the life progression cycle through the chakras. The esoteric statement of "wheels of wheels within wheels of fire," is the procession of consciousness, where each chakra is awakened through three successive passages through the Rays of Initiation. This is the pathway of man's balancing his chakras in the threefold flame of spiritual Christ Consciousness seeking to attain Tenth Ray consciousness. Theos, the God Consciousness, is likewise reached in the same manner. The pathway awaits the opening of our consciousness to the I-Thy-Divine, the consciousness we need everyday while we exist on the planet earth. This is the road that takes us into and through the three levels of the heart.

The "I" is the first level of the heart, the "Thy" is the second, and the "Divine" is the third. In acknowledging the "I" consciousness we attune to a higher level of body awareness: blending the spiritual and physical experience in oneness. We direct our energy in a newly focused realm of expression and feeling. Interestingly, when we open ourselves up to change, we are directed in a unique way to facilitate our needed experiences.

The first level of the heart is the third chakra. This chakra has many functions: will, ego, fear, defense and desire to control our physical body. The first learning experience is to go beyond the past pattern of allowing the third chakra "will" to be directed by the desires of the "I": having to have it my way, by my control, by my power and dominion over all persons and internal functions in my life. At this level of consciousness, the feelings, needs or concerns of others may not have any impact on the "I-ego-ism".

This initial level of growth in the third chakra is from the fear-space attitude: maintaining a defensive approach in a high state of stress within the body. This fear-space precipitates the pattern of reaction, a direct correlation with the mechanism of insecurity, always feeling threatened; therefore, control is seen in the perspective of how to utilize our sense of power. Unfortunately, this perspective is false. The visual field is an illusion due to the emotions distorting the clarity and balance of the brain by disconnecting the right and left hemispheres. This level of functioning is clearly fear dominated and reactionary, which distorts the clarity of the ego functioning in a balanced manner.

This type of domination is very evident in the manipulative, conditional love process: you may have, only if you do as I say and/or desire. What the person is saying by not stating the truth is, "I will love you only if you do as I desire and say." Conditional love pervades our society on all levels from the home, to the government, and all other competition-based organizations such as churches and schools. They often approach philosophical and moral standards from a position of dogmatic logic.

The attitude of conditional love is a lower level of consciousness that we need to transcend before change can take place within the systems of organizations. Organizations are simply the by-product of the individuals who establish and run them. The planetary consciousness functioning from conditional love is between 80-90% of the world population. Our planet requires a transformation of consciousness if change is to take place; however, change begins with our personal integration of love on an unconditional level. When personal change occurs, then we will see planetary shifts. Waiting around for someone else or a government to make change is not where the responsibility lies. It lies in the heart of each soul upon the planet earth.

Each individual must remove the false shields that blind us from seeing clearly if we are to transform this fear into unconditional love. This requires seeing ourselves as unlimited human beings on the planet earth. We need to reject the limitations projected upon us by others. Already these limitations have become unknowingly impregnated into our subconscious. To judge another person is not our privilege.

To achieve this new consciousness, we need to eliminate words like "I cannot" from our vocabulary. Realize that a truthful statement with a positive energy is "I do not desire to expend the energy at this time." We also need to eliminate the word "but" after a statement of action or a thought you "think" you support. The word "but" negates the preceding positive statement, where "and" connects a positive energy. Create a positive statement of spiritual-physical wholeness by saying "I AM" rather than "I". "I AM" is how God described himself to Moses. He said, "I AM THAT I AM." And so are you and I. By saying "I AM" you invoke movement from the lower heart, the third chakra emotional center, into the physical heart, the fourth chakra center. Our statements must be affirmed actively by living the "I AM" for transformation to take place.

Then our intellect begins to actuate an "I AM" consciousness. From this point the "I-ego-ism" begins the journey to fully eliminate itself from our lower heart center, our body, and emotions. The process is a total realignment of the psychological patterns of the collective unconscious mind down to the subconscious and out of our conscious actions and thought processes. Personal transformation is initiated.

When we begin to study a new subject, the definitions must first be learned and then understood in the proper context of their unique relationship with the new subject. The same is true when we begin our path seeking spiritual enlightenment. New words and definitions are presented on an esoteric level to be integrated into the exoteric level of daily existence. We are told that, "there are no accidents and what we put out we get back" and we ask ourselves, "what do these words mean?" We are told that these are statements of universal law, a law that is constant on all levels of human and cosmic consciousness, whether or not we perceive it.

What a new way of thinking! It is foreign to our intellectual and emotional response system. Fortunately, we begin to grasp the concepts of these new definitions and to integrate them into the process of living spiritually. Then God, with a unique sense of humor, provides a confrontation to see if these laws have truly become incorporated in our lives or are simply words spouted from our lips. The truth becomes evident only if these definitions are no longer just words, for then they have been intellectually and emotionally integrated: existing in our emotional response mechanism, our heart. At this point we begin to utilize the esoteric truth of these statements in our daily existence.

This begins the establishment of a new consciousness in our behavior and sets us on a proper course of growth: a continuous spherical expansion of our consciousness bubble. We know that either we are living the true concepts of unconditional love, or that we have not grown beyond the limiting emotions of fear.

Another shift that must take place in the movement from the third chakra into the fourth chakra of the heart is to learn the process of surrender. This is really the major process of the heart learning to manifest the threefold flame of unconditional love.

Surrender does not mean to be a doormat to be stepped on by everyone. It requires the clarity to see distinctly that your rights are as important as everyone else's; however, by loving yourself, you love and respect the rights of others. To surrender is to not manipulate another, or groups, from one's desire to control; it is the allowance of another's needs to have equal priority. It is the creation of the "Win-Win," rather than the accustomed "Win-Lose" state of survival through competition.

It is at this level of consciousness that the ego is flowing in the Love-Will-Wisdom Ray, the higher vibrations of the third chakra. A peaceful state of being pervades our process of living. When this has fully occurred on all levels of consciousness within our lives, then the "I will" transforms into "Thy will." "Thy will be done on earth, not mine." When we realize that our true will is "Thy Will" and that surrender is not a sacrifice, then the expansion takes on another dimension. The unconditional love Self provides the vehicle for the God Consciousness, or the Divine level of the heart, to manifest in our lives.

Awareness of "Divine Will," housed within the fabric of our heart, comes to light. The higher vibrations of the eighth chakra, the etheric heart chakra, begins to resonate within our thoughts, words, and feelings. An entirely new process is conceived without effort, for it simply evolves as a direct proponent of the consciousness bubble expansion.

The Rays of Progression, our initiations through the twelve levels of consciousness, are correspondent to our process of expansion in consciousness; however, the Rays progress in a constant order. This progression is activated by freewill and the conscious decision that we desire to embrace the spiritual teachings. The speed of completion of each level is, likewise, dependent upon our ability to fly into the fires of initiation.

This progression through the Personality Rays begins with the First Ray and ends with the Seventh Ray. The pathway through each Ray of initiation begins with activating the root chakra and is completed when the Crown Chakra is reached. We are allowed the experiences of integrating each chakras' lessons, and are nurtured in the focused radiation of the Ray.

When we are progressing from the First through the Third Rays, we are learning the lessons to open the "I-ego-ism" to the consciousness of the "I AM" will. These first three Rays correspond to the fifth chakra, third chakra, and Creative Distributor, respectively. In the First Ray, the opening of the throat center to the transmissions from the higher conscious self begin to purify the actions of the desire body in the Second Ray, focused in the solar plexus center. Then we progress into the Third Ray, where we are focused on the creative centers of the sacrum and spleenic centers, and the new concepts of universal unconditional love begin to transform these complex centers.

At this point in our expansion of consciousness, we experience what appears to be a continuous stream of tests on our journey through the path of spirituality, most often not clearly understood in the proper context. We will first consider that "an unknown or known person" is placing walls before us to impede our progress. What must be fully accepted at this crossroads is that you, the individual, place in front of you the needed lessons to achieve enlightenment. God does not punish you. God grants all of your wishes and affirms all of your feelings, thoughts, and statements about yourself. If you say "I can," then God will affirm with "Yes, you can." However, the reverse is equally true: if you say, "I cannot," then you will not.

It is with the completion of these three Rays that we truly begin the intense cycle of growth. The first cycle now completed dealt with the redirection of the "I" into comprehending the meaning of "Will." It is the remaining cycles where the true test of spiritual growth is confronted.

The entrance into the Fourth Ray of initiation is not simply by desire. It requires a commitment of our total self: a commitment that spans all of the levels of the Etheric Bodies to the cosmic consciousness hidden within the collective unconsciousness of the soul memory. When we evidence an intense soul commitment to move forward in our journey, we are invited by the master of the Fourth Ray to enter his level of initiation.

If we are offered the fourth initiation and accept, then we realize that there is no turning back on the spiritual path during the remainder of this life. This is a major point in the evolution of the soul beyond the astral level where we were more easily subject to the influences of the Dark Brotherhood. However, this does not mean that we are free from the attempts of the Dark Brotherhood to redirect our energies. In fact, the presence of the Dark Forces are even more attracted to the Light Workers than those who might be somewhere between in their soul path.

Now, during this period of growth in the Fourth Ray we continue to learn the true application of these previously learned definitions. Furthermore, we learn the needed discipline during this spiraled expansion through the crystal of the heart. The Fourth Ray is the fourth chakra and through which the twelve pastel petals of the heart must be illumined. These twelve petals can be likened unto the twelve houses of the horoscope.

Completion of the Fourth Ray leads then into the Fifth Ray of divine love, the Ray of the etheric heart, the eighth chakra. This Ray deals with seeking truth, but not in a scientific or intellectual manner. It is the development of learning to listen and feel with the divine or higher heart chakra. We learn a most crucial and important lesson from which enlightenment stems: how to distinguish the truth from the illusion. This process is a continued purification of the senses that have developed from the beginning of the journey in expanded consciousness. As we continue our journey the senses become more refined to the subtlety of Maya, which presents us with the question "What is the reality of the illusion and the illusion of the reality?" Our progression through the Rays continues, developing the senses of our higher consciousness and the devotion to our mission on the planet earth during this lifetime.

A statement needs to be clearly made in reference to the Dark Brotherhood. The teachings of the Dark Brotherhood are oriented for the sole development of power for the sake of power. It is the "I-ego-ism" of the third chakra that seeks power and control for the satisfaction of the self; it is greed; it is all that is not of God's light. *Most importantly, the teachings of the Dark Forces resemble those of the Light Forces on the surface; the distinction comes in the application of the teachings.* The Dark Forces are for self only. Light Forces are for the betterment of humankind, which requires the application of the Servant Self to accomplish growth. It is here that the development of clarity in the heart is most important. Clear spiritual discernment is crucial.

Be a clear vessel so that the light can radiate fully through your life. Know that greed, disrespect for the rights of others, conditional love and manipulation allows the fear center to be the controlling factor in your life. These are, of course, only a few functions of the lower "I" self.

Initiation into the spiral of spiritual expansion of your consciousness bubble is totally up to you. Whether you seek to attune to the lower ego consciousness, or aspire to challenge yourself to being accepted into the Fourth Ray, is not a point to judge. You must remember that you will aspire to the potential that you set for yourself and chose before your birth.

You can never take the position to force the will of another person or group consciousness. Each soul must make his own decision; whether you give your power away to another person or keep it yourself, your freewill created either action.

Each soul has the freewill to choose what it desires during its incarnation on the planet earth. The proper application of universal laws, such as the teachings of the masters of the White Brotherhood, the Angelic Kingdom and all other realms that embrace and teach the truth of light, God's true unconditional love, frees you from the Maya.

The I-Thy-Divine aspect of our living consciousness is an evolutionary process that does not have a specified point of completion. Each of us learns that evolution means to make continued evolvement. My understanding of the word evolvement is a working definition of life. Each day we have choices to make. Each day we are faced with minor and major crossroads, and depending upon our choice we change the present and the potential of the future. The basis for our decisions are either in harmony with our Higher Self and the decisions are easy, or the decisions challenge our present understanding of life due to a conflicting point of reference stored in our brain. In the latter situation, we must draw upon our intuitive or survival mechanisms to make the choice.

Our point of reference clearly defines the continuous stage of refining and implementing our highest potential of I-Thy-Divine consciousness. Since our life is a complex multitude of levels of experiences, we do not always maintain the continuity of a single consciousness throughout the day. Each challenge must, however, be recognized as a golden opportunity to reach for divine level of consciousness. Gaining understanding and expanding a little more each day into the God Consciousness by manifesting the I AM self in all that we do and say is our objective.

Chapter 10

More About *Reiki Plus* Philosophy

The Do's of Reiki Plus

We must remember that all that ever was, is. Nothing is new; only our awareness has expanded. We can bring the inner truth of the words into the reality of our everyday feeling and lifestyle. The more we do this, the closer we are with God, and the closer we are to the truth of ourselves. It is truth that humankind searches for through the manifested form of the flesh. Follow the heart without the misdirection of the desires and you will stand beside truth. Life is a journey in evolving to understand the human display and sharing of love. We can be resourceful and take the first four letters of the word evolve, *evol,* and place them in reverse to create the word *love.* It is a known truth of the spiritually minded aspirant that love is the basis of life's learning and likewise in learning to love we evolve.

Do accept God's unconditional divine love and forgiveness. Forgive yourself for your "sins" and for holding yourself in a state of guilt, or you will always see yourself in a state of limitation and imperfection.

Do remember that it is not that you fall down, it is the attitude with which you stand up that is important. Forgive yourself and the person(s) who participated in your falling down, and then thank them for participating in the growth experience. For without them there would have been no growth.

Do know that God allows us to learn from each opportunity with which we choose to challenge ourselves. Clarify the confusion caused by the emotional self by surrendering your pain to your heart. You will hear the truth through a clear mental body, where harmony between the left and right hemispheres resonates wholeness.

Do follow your intuition and you will soar like the eagle.

Do accept the love within yourself and manifest God's creative force in all that you think, say, and do.

Do radiate the healing energy of Reiki at all times: sending healing to self and others.

Do follow the Five Spiritual Principles of Reiki: Just for Today...

Do know that the client is the true healer: God allows us the opportunity to witness His miracles.

Do await the client to ask for healing; but know that at times you need to invite the person to open the door.

Do remember that all who knock of their own accord will be most eager to enter the Garden of Eden.

Do know the difference between the sincere and insincere desire of the client to take personal responsibility.

Do affirm yourself as a channel of love, showing the compassion of unconditional love through honesty to all who perpetuate their personal struggle by desiring sympathy or indulging in tactics of manipulation.

Do know that you are an endless well of love; share this unlimited bounty with all creations living on Mother Earth and directing the light from Father Sun.

Do see yourself rewarded, happy, and prosperous. Reach out and accept God's abundance.

Do bless all expressions of prosperity that come through you from God; remember that earthly prosperity is only a parallel of spiritual prosperity: God's blessing to you for doing His work.

Do know that all gifts given in the true spirit of love are returned tenfold or more.

Share the love in your heart and you will know the joys of God's treasures on earth as they are in heaven.

Your List of Do's:

READING LIST

TITLE	AUTHOR
Reiki Plus Natural Healing	David G. Jarrell
The Initiate Trilogy	Cyril Scott
All books by	Dr. Emmet Fox
All books by	Neville
The Lamsa Holy Bible, and all books by	George Lamsa
The Prophet, and all books by	Kahlil Gibran
Women's Bodies, Women's Wisdom	Christiane Northrup, MD
Zen Flesh, Zen Bones	Paul Reps
Joshua, and all other books by	Father Girzone
Occult Anatomy And The Bible	Corinne Heline
All books by	Dane Rudhyar
All Astrological book by	Alan Leo
All Astrological books by	Sakolan & Acker
The Peaceful Warrior	Dan Millman
The Impersonal Life, and all books by	J. S. Banner
The Tao of Pooh	Benjamin Hoff
All White Eagle and Silver Birch Books	Grace Cooke
Jonathan Livingston Seagull and Illusions	Richard Bach
Old Time Remedies, and other books by	Rev. Hanna Kroeger
The Colon Health Handbook	Robert Gray
All books by	Bernard Jensen,D.C.
Indian Herbology Of North America	Alma R. Hutchens
All books by	Dr. John R. Christopher
The Biochemic System Of Medicine	George Carey, M.D.
How To Get Well	Paavo Airola, Ph.D.
Vitamin Bible	Earl Mindella, R.Ph.
Food Is Your Best Medicine	Henry G. Bieler, M.D.
Encyclopedia of Medical Astrology	H.L.Cornell, M.D.
The Kingdom Of The Shining Ones	Flower Newhouse

A Course In Miracles	Found. for Inner Peace
Thought Power, and other books by	Annie Besant
Law Of Life Book I & II	A. D. K. Luk Pub.
Love Is Letting Go Of Fear	Gerald Jampolsky, M.D.
Handbook To Higher Consciousness	Ken Keyes
All books by	C. W. Leadbeater
Touch For Health	John Thie, D.C.
Your Body Doesn't Lie	Dr. John Diamond, M.D.
Vibrational Medicine	Dr. Gerber
Nutritional Vitamin Therapy	Dr. Michael Lesser, M.D.
The Merck Manual	Merck Publications
The Little Herb Encyclopedia	Jack Ritchason, N.D
Prescription for Nutritional Healing	Balch & Balch
Foundations of Health	Christopher Hobbs
On Common Ground	Dr. Philip Fritchey, N.D.
Healing the Child Within	Charles L. Whitfield, MD
Life And Teachings Of The Master Of The Far East	Baird T. Spalding series

Chapter 11

Specific Imbalances

This book is directed at the integrated healing of the human psycho-physical organism, from the approach of harmonizing the mind, body, and emotions, and increasing the receptivity of light from Spirit.

The information contained in this chapter is solely for the purpose of education. It is the intent of the ***Reiki Plus Institute*** to provide the highest degree of holistic health care education available; therefore, **the diagnosing, prescribing, and treatment of disease must be left to the licensed physician, chiropractor, and psychologist.** Your objective as a health care facilitator is to establish a working relationship with the medical practitioner to cooperatively treat the client.

As you seek the level of professionalism inherent to your dedication in spiritual holistic health care, we trust that you will always accept the divine guidance from God spoken through many portals as well as your own. The wellness of your client is of the utmost importance, not your ego.

The books listed below were used as reference material for the following chapter. Please refer to these books for more detailed information:

1. *How To Get Well,* Paavo Airola, Ph.D., N.D.
2 *School of Natural Healing,* Dr. John Christopher, N.D., Herbal Pharmacist degree.
3. *The Biochemic System of Medicine*, George W. Carey, M.D.
4. *Vitamin Bible,* Earl Mindell, Pharm. B., R.Ph.
5. *Reiki Plus Natural Healing,* David G. Jarrell,
6. *On Common Ground*, Dr. Philip Fritchey, N.D.
7. *Prescriptions for Health*, Balch and Balch
8. *The Little Herb Book*, Dr. Jack Ritchason

How to Use This Chapter's Information

The most common physical and emotional disorders responsive to the healing energy and practice of Reiki are presented in this chapter. Please realize that the depth and breath of physiological and psychological disorders that challenge human and animal kind is broad, and beyond the scope of this book. We hope that the chosen disorders contained in this chapter will serve you educationally to better understand the phenomena of the disorder.

Imbalance: the name of the disorder is given;

Manifestation: describes how this disorder manifests itself in the body; this section also contains the symptoms commonly associated with the disorder;

Reiki Treatment: all disorders require a full body treatment to establish harmony to the body; however, where appropriate specific parts of the anatomy, glandular system, skeletal and muscular systems are mentioned because they will probably require additional healing energy. Treatment procedures other than Reiki are referenced because the 33 years of combined healing experience have proven to the authors that certain disorders require a specific treatment plan to best align the client's energy to speed the healing.

- ***PSEB (Physio-Spiritual Etheric Body Healing)***: is the alignment of the biomagnetic energy bodies surrounding all living systems. The electric impulses of the physical body are regulated and created by this magnetic field. When an etheric body is out of synchronization, the functional imbalance is registered in the anatomy and physiology of the person.
- ***Psycho-Therapeutic Reiki Plus***: this technique uses a specific energy field that can be created with Second Degree Reiki energy to allow the client to find the hidden seed memories now manifested within the anatomy. ***Psycho-Therapeutic Reiki Plus*** allows the practitioner to assist the client's uncovering the true casual factor(s) underlying the mind-body-emotional disconnect. It is a professional procedure that requires a series of sessions to thoroughly clear the psycho-physical, psycho-mental and psycho-emotional distortions. It is available in our Home Study Program on audio cassette.
- ***SAT***: is the Spinal Attunement Technique for somatic and meningeal memory release from the central nervous system to align the spine and establish sacral-cranial balance. This technique uses Second Degree energy in a specific manner and is open to all students of Second Degree Reiki.
- ***Esoteric Psychology and Anatomy:*** a class which presents an understanding of the mystical in the physical world of psychology and anatomy as they pertain to the mind-body-emotion disconnection from spirit and the resulting manifestation of disease.

Nutritional Needs:

Foods: detrimental and beneficial to the chemical balance of the body suffering from the specific disorder. One non-food the body needs more than any other is pure water to cleanse it, and as an energy conductor. Water containing any substance or additive other than lemon juice is processed by the body and kidneys as food. Most individuals do not drink an adequate amount of water each day.

Vitamins, Minerals and Herbs: known to support the chemical balancing and supplementation of the body. The best source is from organic substances or from organic gardening. If quantitative amounts are listed, this does not suggest nor authorize you to recommend this dosage to the client. Proper nutritional testing performed by a qualified and licensed practitioner can insure correct selection and quantity needed.

Special Nutritional/Herbal Combinations: combinations that have been found to support the nutritional needs of the body. Please contact the authors directly for further information about these combinations.

Homeopathic Tissue Salts: the twelve Tissue Salts developed in the 1800's by Dr. W.H. Schuessler. They are available in 6X, 12X and 30X dosages. Homeopathic treatment seeks to provide the substance to support the need of the body rather than attack the symptom.

Medical Referral: the medical support needed to provide acute health care treatment and to provide diagnostic testing, prescribe MRI or CAT scans or other laboratory testing necessary to understand the physiological dimensions of the client's disorder.

Environmental changes needed: daily or habitual patterns that need altering in the life of the client

Probable Esoteric Psychological Relationship: an attempt to provide you with information that might apply to the psycho-dynamics challenging the client's personality and soul. Please do not attempt nor consider that these words, phrases or indicators will fit all persons having the disorder. This is not the intent of this information. Kahlil Gibran clearly states in his book *The Prophet*, "And if you would know God be not therefore a solver of riddles."

Please do not consider that a metaphysical interpretation is always accurate or supportive to the healing process. If the metaphysical information is divinely oriented and the person is at least a neophyte aspirant seriously accepting his or her role as solely responsible for life's drama, then this level of information can be insightful. On the other hand, however, if the client is purely a neophyte to the inner-dimensional workings of the spiritual realm, this approach will simply be considered illogical and irrational.

It is immature and irresponsible to presume that you or anyone else, other than the person's soul and God, has the answer to fix the problem.

The psycho-mental, psycho-physical and psycho-emotional

dynamics of the soul are complexly entwined in the actions of the personality's freewill choices often from a long term pattern of behavior. There is not simply an easy answer to many of life's challenges.

The information listed in this section refers to the anatomical parts affected, the chakra centers and the etheric bodies that are carrying the biomagnetic imbalances, showing the improper electrical conductivity in this area of the body. For all practical purposes of observation these etheric imbalances may not be obvious to the Practitioner untrained in *PSEB*.

Definitions of Terms Used in this Chapter

Chakra: a vortex of spiraling energy surrounding the physical anatomy. Called a chakra body by the authors. For in-depth information you are invited to study the healing technique *PSEB* which is a class oriented to chakra balancing.

Chakra Center: the gland in the endocrine system or body part where the biomagnetic energy of the chakra registers in the physiology, and from which it stimulates the center to distribute the hormones or life force into the body.

Etheric Body: a chakra, also known as a chakra body. Each chakra body is the same as the corresponding etheric body.

CDC: Creative Distributor Center, the sacrum, where the Cosmic Fire entering through the eighth Etheric body (eighth chakra) flows down the spinal cord into the coccyx, the kundalini center, and is then distributed from the sacrum through the central nervous system if there is no interference from psycho-mental, psycho-physical and psycho-emotional imbalances in the system.

Anti-Rotational Body: the chakra bodies rotate in a clockwise rotation for the right-handed person and counter-clockwise for the left handed person. An anti-rotation therefore means a body in the opposite rotation, that may result in great psycho-mental, psycho-physical and psycho-emotional disorders in the associated physiology controlled by the anti-rotational body.

Vitamin E normalizes the blood pressure. It is recommended that Vitamin E be taken daily for many disorders. Please note that the safe way to do so it to begin with a dosage of 100 I.U.'s daily for 7 days, then to increase 100 I.U.'s weekly. Vitamin E needs Vitamin A and C to properly metabolize. These three are powerful anti-oxidants.

Vitamin C: ascorbic acid for bacterial infections and to remove the acid pH towards alkaline pH; ascorbate, normally combined with a mineral, is for viral infections and to remove the alkaline pH towards acid pH.

Alphabetical Listing of Specific Imbalances

Imbalance: Abortion—Emotional and Physical Residue

***(also see* Menstrual disorders)**

Manifestation: Sexual imbalances, irregular periods, abnormal Pap smears, infertility or the inability to be emotionally and/or physically open to your spouse/partner.

Reiki Treatment: Full body to help any physical discomfort.

- *Psycho-Therapeutic Reiki Plus* to treat the deep layers of unresolved guilt between the mother and the unborn child. The trauma is normally greater than supposed, since the mother mentally justified her actions due to the prevailing circumstances leading to the decision. Forgiveness on all five layers will be necessary to clear the causal energy contained in the reproductive system and the heart.
- *PSEB* Advanced is a great assistance in aligning and releasing the deeply buried memory of an abortion.
- *SAT* if the trauma implanted in the sacrum and/or the spinal column creating pain or spinal misalignment.

Chakra Centers: First, second, fourth and sixth

Imbalance: Accidents

Manifestation: Physical injury

Reiki Treatment: Check for breathing, bleeding, and shock.

- Have someone call 911 if the injury is serious.
- If not breathing, administer artificial respiration.
- Then to prevent or neutralize shock, place one hand on adrenal glands or solar plexus or the head (for stabilizing the pituitary, pineal and hypothalamus glands and balancing the brain functions.) If you can not reach the third chakra center, then place both hands on the head in position #2. *(Do not move an injured victim - spinal injury may have occurred.)*
- Bleeding or injured area: use compress and wear plastic glove to prevent skin coming into contact with the victim's blood if pressure is need on the wound to stop the bleeding. Otherwise, place hand over the injury and dressing until symptoms are stabilized. *PSEB* for the fourth body.
- Once assistance is rendered you may never leave or stop treatment until relieved by a medical or para-medical person.

- If unable to reach or assist the injured person then treat with Absentia.

Nutritional Needs:
- Foods: None are to be given.
- Herbs: Special Note: If you are trained in the use of herbs, Fo-Ti is an excellent stabilizer for the chakras; Rescue Remedy of the Bach flower essences also stabilizes the body energy. If no medical personnel are available and you have the need to eliminate deep lingering pain, valerian root is very effective; however, it is a very powerful herb: 5-8 drops of tincture or one capsule for pain as needed. Valerian will assist the Reiki by allowing the person to rest deeply. Do Not administer valerian to a victim who has suffered spinal, cranial, internal, or respiratory injury, they need medical attention.

Medical Referral: Any person having suffered injury from an accidental cause needs to receive diagnostic evaluation to ensure proper medical care is given.

Probable Esoteric Psychological Relationship: It is considered that an injury to the self draws the individuals attention to the functional relationship between the body part and its esoteric functions and meaning. We refer you to the course of study *Esoteric Anatomy* that is available by Home Study audiocassettes. Not all injuries or accidents have a metaphysical or hidden message. Accidents can be a simple lack of awareness of what one is doing and not being observant.

Imbalance: ADD/ADHD (See Hyperactivity)

Imbalance: Adhesions

Manifestation: Scar tissue adhering to adjoining tissue resultant from surgery; also from compression of tissue due to overweight or compaction of the intestines and bowels. Infection can contribute from soft tissue trauma due to fluid stagnation.

- Symptoms: Pain in movement at adhesion; bowels, difficulty in movement if adhesions restrict colon.

Reiki Treatment: Treat directly over adhesion or scar.
- *PSEB* to associated chakra body.
- Meditation: visualization of adhesions being eaten away.
-

Nutritional Needs:
- Herbs: licorice.
- Vitamins: A, D, C, and E, B-Complex.
- Minerals: Full Spectrum of minerals.
- Topical application of Vitamin E or Aloe Vera
- Homeopathic Tissue Salts: Silica, Kali Sulf., Ferrum Phos.
- For Sedimentation: 2 tablespoons organic Apple Cider vinegar and 1

tbs. honey.

Imbalance: Aging

Manifestation: Natural physiological process of all living organisms, excess free radical damage.

Reiki Treatment: Complete treatments daily.

- Meditations : regeneration visualization

Nutritional Needs:

- Foods: Balanced nutrition with reduction or elimination of mucoid foods; add fresh or fresh frozen fruits and vegetables; digestive enzymes, lecithin
- Herbs: Female - gota kola, dong quai; male - ginseng. Both sexes: Fo-Ti, gingko.
- Vitamins: A, E, C and a Full spectrum B Complex with amino acids.
- Minerals: Full spectrum.
- Special Nutritional/Herbal Combinations: Brain Formula, Grape Seed/Pine Bark Combination, Colon Cleanse Combination, Build Combination
- Homeopathic Tissue Salts: Multi-Salt (12 tissue salts).

Environmental changes needed: Fresh air, exercise, and yoga.

Imbalance: Alcoholism

- Manifestation: Drinking until incapacitated; drinking to forget.

Reiki Treatment:

- Full body with additional attention to Head positions #1, #2, #3 and adrenal glands and kidneys.
- *Psycho-Therapeutic Reiki Plus* to treat the addictive mental and emotional disorder.
- Meditation extremely important.

Nutritional Needs:

- Foods: Add garlic and acidophilus, and Yin foods; elimination of sugars in all forms. A yeast free diet is essential (See *Yeast Connection*, Dr. Crook). Fasting with supplements.
- Herbs: Red clover and milk thistle to cleanse liver, licorice, kudzu, St. John's wort, evening primrose or black currant oil.
- Vitamins: B-Complex w/amino acids, Vit. C, A, D, and E, up to 1500 mg of L-Glutamine daily, and 250-500 mg Niacinamide has been found effective by medical science.
- Minerals: Full spectrum with Zinc (60 mg), GTF Chromium (Chromium P-colinate), Magnesium
- Special Nutritional/Herbal Combinations: Milk Thistle Blend, Red Clover Combination, Stress Formula, Energy Combination
- Homeopathic Tissue Salts: Silicea, Kali Phos., Mag. Phos., Calcium

Phos.
Medical Referral: Nutritionist and Alcohol Counselor

Environmental changes needed: Social friends and habitats may need evaluation; exercise.

Probable Esoteric Psychological Relationship: Often the result of an unhealed Child Within. Feeling fearful from inability to succeed, self-pity. Directed by the lower passions rather than spiritual unity. An escape mechanism which leads the weak willed or addictive personality into a state of self-induced illusion. Alcoholics often have external attachments from the astral plane and if this is so, will have a spirit possession needing proper release. A tear in the Etheric Bodies is possible with alcoholism. Etheric Surgery is a means to repair this type of tear.

- Body Parts: Liver, adrenal, pancreas, pineal and heart.
-
- Chakra Centers: Third, fourth and seventh.

Imbalance: Allergies

Manifestation: Blood chemistry alkaline, emotional structure sensitive, genetic or acid-base metabolism imbalanced. Ingestion of processed foods with chemical additives. Consumption of foods that trigger the emotional causation to imbalance the biochemistry.

- Symptoms: Reaction to foods over-sensitizing blood chemistry. Oftentimes from feeding foods incapable of assimilation due to lack of proper enzymes during infant period. Breast-feeding builds proper immune strength.

Reiki Treatment:

- Full body; additional time on adrenals, pancreas, liver, thymus, thyroid and spleen;
- *Psycho-Therapeutic Reiki Plus*
- *PSEB*

Nutritional Needs: Fasting to cleanse.

- Foods: Organic chemical free. Eliminate milk (cow's) and wheat, which are often sources of allergens. Need foods rich in manganese. Green leafy vegetables, bananas, and potatoes for potassium.
- Vitamins: Vit. C (mega 5,000 or more daily), Vit A (10-25,000 I.U. beta carotene), D (1,000 I.U.), E (800 I.U., begin with 100 I.U.'s and increase 100 IU's weekly due to potential effect on increasing the blood pressure), B-Complex, Bee Pollen.
- Special Nutritional/Herbal Combinations: Colon Cleanse Combination, Thymus Support Combination, Chinese Digestive Support Blend, Intestinal Repair Combination, Marshmallow Combination, Liver Support Combination, Milk Thistle Blend. Homeopathic Remedies: Allergy, Hay fever/Pollen, Mold/Yeast/Dust.

- Homeopathic Tissue Salts: Kali Phos.
- Digestive Enzymes

Medical Referral: Nutritionist, Naturopath or Homeopathic physician for proper testing of food groups and environmental agents.

Environmental changes needed: As directed by physician, nutritionist.

Probable Esoteric Psychological Relationship: What fear is triggering the ego to react to a person, the environment or "unknown" stimulant of the past so that it can be resolved and forgiven? Resistance to accept your claim for control.

Body Parts: Pancreas, adrenals.

Chakra Centers: Third, fifth and eighth.

Imbalance: Arteriosclerosis

Manifestation: Hardening of the arteries from plaque and hard fats, sugar products are a prime cause of hardening of the arteries.

- Symptoms: Tiredness and general deterioration of the body if prolonged condition exists.

Reiki Treatment: Full body; arms and legs, lungs and heart,

- *Psycho-Therapeutic Reiki Plus* for psycho-emotional, mental and physical seed origins.
- *PSEB* to release deeply imbedded conflicts emotionally.

Nutritional Needs:

- Foods: Eliminate hydrogenated and saturated fats; red meats, salt and processed foods, white flour and sugar. Crucial: Add juices and vegetables, fiber, digestive enzymes.
- Herbs: garlic, cayenne, butcher's broom, golden seal, mistletoe leaves, hawthorn berries, rose hips.
- Vitamins: Lecithin granules, choline, B Complex, Vit A, C, D, E, B3 (Niacin, time-release) and Evening Primrose Oil, l-lysine amino acid.
- Minerals: Cal-mag., multi-minerals, and GTF chromium.
- Special Nutritional/Herbal Combinations: Circulatory Combination, Gingko and Hawthorne Combination, Mineral Combination.
- Homeopathic Tissue Salts: Calc. Fluor.

Medical Referral: Nutritionist, Naturopath, Homeopathic physician, Internist or a Cardiovascular specialist.

Environmental changes needed: Care to prevent metal poisoning from cooking utensils, plumbing and contaminated water. Eliminate smoking, as smoking causes cardiovascular constriction.

Probable Esoteric Psychological Relationship: Closing down the expression of inner self to self and others; narrowing of concepts creating limitation. Hardening of the mind, and limitation of receptivity. The brittle attitude corresponds to the lack of connective tissue in the wall linings, which allows a more flexible manner of living and giving. The cell salt calcium fluoride increases the connective tissue and the elasticity of the wall linings.

Body Parts: Heart, arteries.

Chakra Centers: Fourth, eighth.

Imbalance: Arthritis, Rheumatoid

Manifestation: Acid balance too high. Deposits of calcium in tissue at joint affected. Now considered to be a classification of auto-immune disorders.

- Symptoms: Pain and swollen joints and tendons.

Reiki Treatment:

- Full; affected joints. Additional on Immune complex (Thyroid, Thymus and Spleen), kidneys, bladder, and base of spine.
- *SAT* if located in the spine, or *Psycho-Therapeutic Reiki Plus* if in the limbs or client uncomfortable in prone (face down) position.
- *PSEB.*

Nutritional Needs:

- Foods: Eliminate acid foods (Yang). Add: Lemon water (10 or more 8 oz. glasses daily, except at mealtime), increase vegetables: raw, juices, alfalfa sprouts.
- Herbs: yucca, morinda, hydrangea, Irish moss, burdock, parsley, alfalfa, dandelion
- Vitamins: C (3-5000 mg ascorbic acid), K (potassium), B3 (Niacinamide), B6 (50-100 mg), pantothenic acid (100 mg), B-Complex, E (600-1000 I.U -- begin with 100 I.U. per week and increase 100 I.U.'s per week due to increase of blood pressure). Pre-emulsified Cod liver oil, 1 tbs. daily taken two and one half hours after a meal for pain.
- Minerals: Cal-mag. (2:1 ration); multi.
- Special Nutritional/Herbal Combinations: Joint & Structural Combination, Ayurvedic Joint Blend, Chinese Inflammation Combination, MSM Combination Cream, Natural Pain Relief Combination, Progesterone Cream Combination.

Medical Referral: Nutritionist, chiropractor for spinal, massage therapist, medical physician.

Probable Esoteric Psychological Relationship: Resentment and anger. Restriction of receiving or giving; taking responsible action to fulfill potentials and goals. Unconscious desire to create immobility, depositing of crystallized thoughts at the affected body parts. Creative expression necessary.

Body Parts: Kidneys, bladder, kundalini center, inflamed or crippled body part.

Chakra Centers: First, second, third, fourth and fifth.

Imbalance: Arthritis, Osteo

Manifestation: Alkaline balance too high. Deterioration of cartilage of joints.

- Symptoms: Immobility at pained joints; weakening of skeletal structure.

Reiki Treatment: Full; affected body parts,

- *Psycho-Therapeutic Reiki Plus* or *SAT* to release the psycho - physical and emotional charge.
- *PSEB*.

Nutritional Needs:

- Foods: Increase Yang foods. Use organic apple cider vinegar, 1 tbsp. daily to increase body acid metabolism.
- Herbs: yucca, morinda, anamu, una de gato, hydrangea, Irish moss, burdock, parsley, alfalfa, dandelion, safflower
- Vitamins: C (3-5000 mg Ascorbate), K (potassium), B3 (Niacinamide),), pantothenic acid (100 mg), B-Complex, E (600-1000 I.U.). Emulsified Cod liver oil, 1 tbsp. daily taken two and one half hours after a meal for pain.
- Minerals: Cal-mag. (1:2 ration) B6 (50-100 mg in 25 mg dosages to assist the Ca.-Mg); multi.
- Special Nutritional/Herbal Combinations: Joint & Structural Combination, Chinese Inflammation Combination, MSM Combination Cream, Natural Pain Relief Combination, Progesterone Cream Combination, Protein Digestion Combination, Digestive Support Blend, Shark Cartilage Combination.
- Homeopathic Tissue Salts: Ferrum Phos., Nat. Sulf., and Nat. Phos.

Medical Referral: Nutritionist, chiropractor for spinal, massage therapist, medical physician.

Probable Esoteric Psychological Relationship: Passive state of anger-resentment which has reached an attitude of "why even try." Redirection of goals and self-love is necessary. The overly critical personality often accompanies the arthritic disorders.

Body Parts: Kidneys, bladder, inflamed or crippled body part.

Chakra Centers: First, Creative Distributor, second, third, fourth, fifth and eighth.

Imbalance: Asthma

Manifestation: Allergy and emotional disorders.

- Symptoms: Inability to breathe, wheezing with dry and painful cough due to irritation of mucous membranes in bronchial tubes.

Reiki Treatment: Full body, lungs.

- 21 days of continuous treatment is required treating with First Degree and possibly with Second Degree hands on. Throat, solar plexus, adrenals, and base of spine will be affecting physiology.
- Once client is asymptomatic and stable, then *Psycho-Therapeutic Reiki Plus* is effective in releasing the deep seated emotions.

Nutritional Needs:
- Foods: Elimination of all mucous-forming: dairy (milk) products, eggs, wheat, rye, oats, grains, sugar, caffeine, chocolate, meat, pasta. Add fruits and vegetables, juices, and water, flax seed oil
- Need to clean the bowels and lymphatic system.
- Herbs: cayenne, fenugreek, aloe vera, mullein; lobelia, valerian with cayenne excellent for spasm. Garlic.
- Vitamins: A, E, C, D, B6 (a natural antihistamine), Bee Pollen.
- Minerals: Multi; B6.
- Special Nutritional/Herbal Combinations: Colon Cleanse Combination, Build Combination, Chinese Lung Formula, Allergy & Lung Combination, Lung Expectorant Combination, Ayurvedic Lung Formula
- Homeopathic Tissue Salts: Kali Phos. for breathing; Kali Mur for mucus; Natr. Sulf. - eliminates moisture.

Medical Referral: Nutritionist, Physician, Chiropractor.

Environmental changes needed: Needs dry, fresh air; mild exercise such as yoga to build breathing strength.

Probable Esoteric Psychological Relationship: Feeling overly suffocated by a parent: too much love, love not shown to spouse. The love given is often restrictive in its delivery and essence. The personality of the asthmatic is overly sensitive and often very creative, but not understanding how to release the creativity productively. We see the sense of self-worth and self-esteem in need of being developed by positive results of their creative talents. Unexpressed emotions and feelings also are causal in this disorder. Emotional and nervous disorder, genetic.

Body Parts: Lungs, throat, adrenals, heart, thymus, bowels.

Chakra Centers: Third, fourth, fifth, and eighth.

Imbalance: Auto Immune Disorders (AIDS, HIV, CMV, CFS, Epstein Barr)

- Symptoms: For HIV, pneumocystic pneumonia, Karposi's sarcoma skin cancer, tuberculosis. Otherwise, chronic fatigue, lack of strength, wasting away. See Exhaustion.

The HIV virus may present numerous contaminate problems: Candida (oral thrush); Cytomeglovirus (CMV) causing blindness, mental disturbances ranging from simple short-term memory loss to severe dementia, atypical hormones, liver and toxicity problems as the disease progresses to terminal stages. Recurrent cycles of abnormally high temperatures in the 103°- 106°.

Reiki Treatment:
- Full body, with additional time spent checking the liver, lungs, immune complex and adrenals.
- *Psycho-Therapeutic Reiki Plus* for the emotional challenges.
- *PSEB* to align the anti-rotations of the appropriate chakra body

Nutritional Needs:
- Foods: Avoid sugars, caffeine, alcohol and recreational drugs. Reduce red meat, pork, dairy, and eggs. Add: Fresh organic vegetables, sprouts and fruit (that are not prone to carry mold, i.e., citrus or cantaloupes, which have a rough rind to trap the mold growth). Consider parasite cleanse. Add digestive enzymes.
- Herbs: echinacea, Pau D'Arco, garlic, golden seal, ginkgo, ginseng (male) and dong quai (women), aloe, una de gato.
- Vitamins: B Complex, Vitamin A (beta-carotene), C, and E. Fresh organic juices from carrots, beets and celery to stimulate and enhance the immune system, CoQ10.
- Minerals: Multi
- Special Nutritional/Herbal Combinations: Immune Blend, Immune System Combination, Detoxification Blend, Lymph System Support Blend, Lymph Homeopathic, Colon Cleanse Combination, Chinese Parasite Cleanse, Thymus Support Combination.
- Homeopathic Tissue Salts Kali Phos., Mag. Phos.,Silicea, Ferrum Phos.

Medical Referral: Specialist.

Probable Esoteric Psychological Cause: Extreme separation of the self from God. Guilt and lack of self-forgiveness and self-approval combined with internalized anger consumes the self by destroying the immune complex. The thymus is the corespondent gland to the eighth chakra, the Godself, whose key word is trust and the allowance of God's love to be accepted.

Body Parts: Thyroid, thymus and spleen.

Chakras Centers: All, with special conflict in the Creative Distributor, second, and sixth.

Imbalance: Back Pain (see Spinal Disorder)

Manifestation: Lower back and neck are correspondent to total spinal alignment. See spinal diagram for list of potential physical disorders.
- Symptoms: Pain; immobility of movement in affected area. Lower back: female disorders, constipation, sciatica, etc. Upper neck: headaches, numbness in arms and hands, visual disorders, etc.

Reiki Treatment:

- Entire spinal column and the adjacent muscles attaching to the spine, use *SAT* to remove the trauma stored in the tissue, muscles, ligaments and skeletal system of the spine; also *Psycho-Therapeutic Reiki Plus*.

Nutritional Needs:

- Foods: See specific disorders.
- Vitamins: B-Complex
- Minerals: Multi, especially chelated calcium and magnesium in a powder for quick absorption.
- Herbs: lobelia relaxes muscles, valerian root relaxes nerves.
- Special Nutritional/Herbal Combinations: Bone Combination, Skeletal Builder, Chinese Bone Support, Chinese Inflammation Combination, Herbal Back Adjustment Blend, Joint & Structural Combination, MSM Combination Cream.
- Homeopathic Tissue Salts: Kali Phos., Mag. Phos., Silicea, Calc. Fluor.
- Hydro-Therapy is most beneficial. Adding Epsom Salts and Calcium Lactate to the bath also treats the muscles.

Medical Referral: DNFT Chiropractic (Directional Non-Force Therapy) or Network Chiropractic. Network Chiropractic treatment may not specifically treat for the elimination of pain or manipulate the spine. It is normally their philosophy that the pain is essential to motivate the client through the healing. The Network Chiropractor is not normally trained to address the psycho-emotional-mental-physical conflict.

Environmental Changes Needed: Walking and yoga are two of the best physical exercises to rebuild the muscle strength of the individual to hold the spine in place. Bones are held in place by muscles and ligaments.

Probable Esoteric Psychological Relationship: Improper posture or vertebral impairment resulting from not resolving and forgiving the burdens of past responsibilities. See the spinal chart in *Reiki Plus Natural Healing* and the specific vertebrae that connect to the chakra centers, the organs and the glands of the body. This knowledge will assist your understanding of the area of the spine that is traumatized or injured. The central nervous system is the conveyer of all of the biomagnetic and electrical impulses within the human body, and is therefore subject to being disrupted by unresolved conflicts and stress.

Imbalance: Baldness

- Symptoms: Loss of hair

Reiki Treatment:

- Take additional time on the head; massage scalp with jojoba oil to increase the blood flow to the hair. Do shoulder stands or lying on slant board twice daily for 10-15 minutes.

Nutritional Needs:

- Foods: Vegetable protein rather than meat protein. Soy foods. Eliminate sugar, salt, tobacco, and alcohol. Eat sesame, sunflower, pumpkin seeds; buckwheat, almonds, whole grains, millet and goat's milk.
- Herbs: horsetail, saw palmetto, nettles, alfalfa, parsley, kelp, fenugreek, onions, cayenne, sage.
- Vitamins: B Complex, high potency (100 mg), B3 (niacin, 100-300 mg time release), pantothenic acid (B5) and lecithin granules, E, A, C, D, biotin.
- Minerals: Multi with trace minerals and amino acids, zinc.
- Special Nutritional/ Herbal Combinations: Hair/Skin/Nail Combination, Male Formula, Soy Capsules
- Homeopathic Tissue Salts: Kali Phos., Silicea, Calc. Phos.

Environmental changes needed: Eliminate wearing of tight hats.

Probable Esoteric Psychological Relationship: Too much worry, mental stress. Genetic through mother's side.

Imbalance: Bladder Disorders

Manifestation: Bacterial growth.

- Symptoms: Pain in elimination; bleeding; infections.

Reiki Treatment:

- Position #4 front and #3-4 back (bladder and kidneys); 2-tsp. apple cider vinegar with 1-tsp. honey in a glass of water at mealtime establishes acid balances.
- *Psycho-Therapeutic Reiki Plus* for the emotional challenges.
- *PSEB* to align the anti-rotations of the appropriate chakra body

Nutritional Needs:

- Foods: Reduce: vegetables and fruits. Drink apple cider vinegar with honey. Drink cranberry juice (without sugar) and black cherry juice. Watermelon and pumpkin seeds provide important food value.
- Herbs: uva ursi (inflammation); parsley (increases urination); chamomile, cramp bark, slippery elm for cystitis; cayenne for bleeding, corn silk and marshmallow are soothing, dandelion to cleanse, devil's claw for leakage, goldenseal as antiseptic, juniper berries.
- Vitamins: B Complex, C (5-10,000 mg), A (25,000-50,000), E.
- Minerals: Multiple.
- Special Nutritional/Herbal Combinations: Chinese Kidney Support, Kidney Tonic, Kidney Blend, Chinese Diuretic Blend, Urinary System Tonic, Cranberry & Buchu Formula, Intestinal Flora Blend.
- Homeopathic Tissue Salts: Calc. Sulf. (inflammation); Kali Phos. (Cystitis), Mag. Phos. (retention, spasms); Kali Mur (cystitis with swelling); Ferrum Phos. (inflammation).

Medical Referral: Urologist.

Environmental changes needed: Eliminating foods, alcohol, and drugs that irritate the urinary tract. Exercise.

Probable Esoteric Psychological Relationship: Holding on to old irritating or angry thoughts and ideas, fear of letting go. Related to kidneys where a person seeks to overbalance and then fears whether they have correct perception. Also, a strong relationship to sexual guilt or feelings of erotic misuse.

Body Parts: Kidneys, bladder, reproductive organs, and heart.

Chakra Centers: First, second, third, and fourth.

Imbalance: Bleeding Gums

Manifestation: Too much acid in blood and a lack of calcium in the tissue.

- Symptoms: Tender when brushing, resulting in bleeding.

Reiki Treatment:

- Mouth and jaw; neck and adrenals.

Nutritional Needs:

- Foods: Eliminate acid foods and fruits. Citrus fruits (alkaline ash); eliminate pineapples and strawberries, high in acid. Increase vegetables.
- Herbs: cayenne, bayberry, white oak bark tightens tissue, plantago.
- Vitamins: C, A, D, E, B Complex. CoQ10 supports gum tissue.
- Minerals: K, multi-minerals, especially chelated calcium combined with magnesium.
- Homeopathic Tissue Salts: Calc. Fluor.

Medical Referral: Dental hygiene may be needed, as the cause may be poor oral cleanliness and plaque.

Probable Esoteric Psychological Relationship: Lack of connectivity in one's life or a control issue. Possible anger or tension at the throat level carried into the connective tissue of the gums: holding on by ones "bite."

Chakras Center: Third, fourth and fifth.

Imbalance: Bleeding - Internal

Manifestation: Injury, accident, ulceration, hemorrhage, aneurysm, etc. Bleeding internally is also a calcium deficiency in the body.

- Symptoms: Swelling, bruising under skin, passing blood through stools or urinary tract, internal pain in a specific area of the cardiovascular system.

Reiki Treatment: Specific area of injury. (See "Accident")

Nutritional Needs:

- Minerals: chelated calcium-magnesium.

- Herbs: If the person is conscious, then cayenne or goldenseal if medical attention is not available. Mullein for bleeding from the bowel tissue.
- Special Nutritional/Herbal Combinations: Kidney support is needed to assimilate Calcium, use herbal Chinese Bone and Kidney Formula to rebuild the tissue. Herbal-based calcium is also needed to promote better uptake of the calcium from the chelated minerals you take.

Medical Referral: Seek immediate medical attention for diagnosis and treatment.

Imbalance: Bowel Congestion (see Constipation)

Imbalance: Brain Damage

Manifestation: Accident, stroke, cancer, genetic, mental illness, fatigue, free radical damage.

Reiki Treatment:

- Entire cranial and associated body parts as related to nature of causation; i.e., cancer: spleen, liver, thymus, adrenals, and head.

Nutritional Needs:

- Foods: Lecithin granules; eliminate processed meats, cured meats, soy sauce, tamari, chili, ketchup, mustard, and other high sodium foods.
- Herbs: parsley, gingko.
- Vitamins: L-Glutamine (strokes and memory loss), Lecithin granules; B12; Kelp choline; B3 niacin.
- Minerals: Eliminate sodium excess; add multi-minerals, trace minerals and amino acids. Zinc is important in mental illness and brain damage.

Medical Referral: Seek appropriate medical testing for diagnosis.

Imbalance: Breast Problems, Female

Manifestation: Lumps, cyst, tumors. The ovaries will also have a direct involvement, since the hormones for the breast are received from the ovaries, which implies that there is a pituitary gland dysfunction.

- Cyst: a sac without an opening, fluid or semi-fluid.; waste material contained in an isolated sac.
- Tumor: abnormal formation of parasitic, non-inflammatory cells or tissue arising from the cells of the host.
- Symptoms: Swollen, tender lumps in breast.

Reiki Treatment:

- Breast, reproductive organs, adrenal glands, and pancreas; spleen, liver, and thymus in malignant growths.

- *PSEB* to realign the biomagnetic body affecting the breast and realign its rotation, then
- *Psycho-Therapeutic Reiki Plus* for the psycho-emotional trauma.
- Hot baths with ground fresh ginger root in a cheesecloth (fist size) with one quarter cup of organic apple cider to promote the lymphatic system to open and drain. Castor oil packs.

Nutritional Needs:

- Foods: Eliminate caffeine, sugar, honey, raisins, heavy meat fats and skin of meat products.
  Eat plenty of fresh garlic or take the odorless form. Juice carrots and beets with ginger root to cleanse lymphatic drainage.
- Herbs: Avoid the estrogenic herbs
  - Cyst: black walnut, burdock, apple cider vinegar.
  - Tumors: bayberry, burdock root, walnut leaves, yellow dock.
- Vitamins: B Complex; pancreatic enzymes; A (50,000 I.U.), E (800 I.U.), C (Ascorbate, 3,000 mg minimum); Shark Cartilage, CoQ10.
- Minerals: Multiple
- Special Nutritional/Herbal Combinations: Essiac Tea, Lymph System Support Blend, Lymph Homeopathic, Infection Formula, Blood Purifying Formula.
- Homeopathic Tissue Salts:
  - Tumors: Kali Mur, Calc. Fluor. and Silicea.
  - Cyst: Calc. Phos. and Silicea.

Medical Referral: OB-GYN physician; Nutritionist, Naturopath, Homeopathic physician.

Probable Esoteric Psychological Relationship: Residual thoughts pertaining to emotional suppression as related to location of cyst or tumor. The breast are receptor and givers of nutriment: the left breast receives or denies being given to, while the right breast gives of denies giving. Very often the imbalance of love being received or given is intertwined in the psycho-emotional, mental and physical conflict held in the body. For further insight, refer to book by Christiane Northrup, MD, *Women's Bodies, Women's Wisdom.*

Chakra Centers: First, second, third, and sixth.

Imbalance: Broken Bones

Manifestation: If victim of an accident in which the spinal column may have suffered injury or break, do not move victim unless properly trained. Call for emergency assistance (see "Accident").

- Symptoms: Bruise, pain to touch or move, immobility of limb or body part, bone puncturing skin (treat for bleeding).
- If caused by weak bone structure, calcium deficiency is present.

Reiki Treatment:
- Treat affected area after the bone has been properly set and placed in a cast. Treat only around the break for pain (and adrenals for prevention of shock) until bone is set. Sandwich break and use polarity positions (pages 74-75 *Reiki Plus Natural Healing*).

Nutritional Needs:
- Foods: Green leafy vegetables high in potassium, calcium, and magnesium.
- Herbs: Irish moss; comfrey leaves directly on swollen area (poultice). Pain and discomfort: valerian.
- Vitamins: B Complex, A, C, D, E.
- Minerals: Multiple, zinc (for promoting healing), chelated Cal.-Mag. (1400-700 mg).
- Special Nutritional/Herbal Combinations: Bone Combination, Skeletal Builder, Joint & Structural Combination, Chinese Inflammation Combination and Chinese Kidney and Bone to promote the assimilation of the calcium you take.
- Homeopathic Tissue Salts: Calc. Phos.

Medical Referral: Immediate medical attention.

Imbalance: Bronchitis (see Asthma)

Manifestation: Acute or chronic inflammation of bronchial membranes.

Reiki Treatment:
- Full body, lungs (see "Asthma"); spleen, liver, and thymus.
- *Psycho-Therapeutic Reiki Plus* for the emotional challenges.
- *PSEB* to align the anti-rotations of the appropriate chakra body

Nutritional Needs: (See Asthma).
- Foods: Eliminate mucous foods; increase juices, water. Juice fasting with supplements to cleanse bowels and help lymphatic system remove dead cells from body.
- Herbs: pleurisy root, comfrey root, cayenne, marshmallow, mullein leaves, golden seal.
- Vitamins: B-Complex high potency, B6, A, E, C (500-1000 mg hourly in acute conditions), D.
- Minerals: Multiple, zinc.
- Special Nutritional/Herbal Combinations: Lung Expectorant Combination, Colon Cleanse Combination.
- Homeopathic Tissue Salts: Ferrum Phos. (Febrile condition), Kali Mur (mucus).

Medical Referral: Physician if fever continues or condition does not improve quickly.

Probable Esoteric Psychological Relationship: Reduction of communication, closure of throat due to unnecessary amount of retained emotional and mental discourses. Esoteric anatomical causal factor: bowels blocked from holding within.

Chakra Centers: Third and fifth.

Imbalance: Burns

Manifestation: From thermal, X-ray, sunburn, fire, cooking.
- Symptoms: Pain, dryness of skin, redness of skin, dehydration, blisters.

Reiki Treatment:
- Hold hands over the burn area(s) until the body no longer pulls energy from the hands, which will be after the pain reduces or completely goes away. The pain will increase at the beginning of the treatment of each area as the body releases the heat and the tissue begins to return to a healthy state.
- Treat the pituitary and adrenals and the immune complex: Thyroid - Thymus - Spleen.
- Apply Aloe Vera or Vitamin E directly on burn area. Cover burns with sterile cloth to keep air from contacting skin; in third degree burns, do not put clothing directly on skin.

Nutritional Needs:
- Foods: Fluids, vegetable juices. Do not allow the person to dehydrate.
- Herbs: comfrey poultice applied to burn and bayberry, aloe vera.
- Vitamins: C, A, E, D, PABA, B-Complex, B6.
- Minerals: Zinc.
- Homeopathic Tissue Salts: Ferrum Phos., Kali Mur, Calc. Sup., and Natr. Phos.; Arnica

Medical Referral: Seek medical care if the burn is second degree or worst to check and treat for potential infections of the area.

Imbalance: Calluses, Feet

Manifestation: Spinal misalignment, improper posture, tight shoes.
- Symptoms: Build up of dead tissue on feet.

Reiki Treatment: Treat area after chiropractic adjustment.
- *SAT* to remove trauma from the spinal column. If untrained in *SAT* treat spinal with the polarity technique taught in *Reiki Plus Natural Healing*.

Nutritional Needs:
- Herbs: chamomile as an ointment.
- Vitamins: E, A.

Medical Referral: Chiropractor, Podiatrist.

Environmental changes needed: Stress inducing factors need to be eliminated.

Probable Esoteric Psychological Relationship: Distribution of emotional load is creating imbalance in the spinal column and therefore body posture.

Imbalance: Cancer

Manifestation: The rapid growth of cells contra to the surrounding tissue, cells and or organ or gland, that feed on the healthy cells they attack.

Reiki Treatment:

- *PSEB* to align the anti rotations of the appropriate chakra body(s) and specific anatomical part(s). First treatment of choice to stabilize the cellular activity registering in the chakra body, release the improper biomagnetic activity and promote cellular change.
- Full body, immune system, liver, pancreas, head and cancerous area (organs); Reiki the arms and legs in the polarity position to stimulate white blood cell production that is developed in the bone marrow.
- *Psycho-Therapeutic Reiki Plus* for the clearing the hidden and unforgiven conflict and anger.

Nutritional Needs:

- Foods: Elimination of meat protein, caffeine, sugars. Diet of fresh carrot juice with beets, fruits, vegetables, grains, nuts, beets - all taken raw and of organic, chemical free origin. Cabbage and Brussels sprouts provide indwells for fighting cancer. Shark Cartilage to restrict blood supply to cancer cells or tumor. Digestive and proteolytic enzymes very important.
- Herbs: Pau D'Arco, chaparral, red clover (blood and liver cleanse), white pond lily, blue flag.
- Vitamins: SOD, all anti-oxidants (A, E, C, D, trace minerals and selenium). High concentrates of B-Complex, A, B3, E, B15 and brewers yeast.
- Minerals: Zinc, multiple, amino acids;
- Special Nutritional/Herbal Combinations: Essiac Tea, Red Clover Combination, Special Formula #1, Pau D'Arco Program, Liver Support Combination #2, Detoxification Blend, Colon Cleanse Combination, Build Combination.
- Homeopathic Tissue Salts: Kali Sulf. (skin); Kali Phos. (pain); Ferrum Phos. (pain); Silicea (swelling, dead tissue removal); Natr. Phos. (tongue).
- For further insight, read *A Cancer Battle Plan* by Anne E. Frähm with David J. Frähm.

Medical Referral: Nutritionist, Naturopath, Homeopathic physician, Oncologist.

Environmental changes needed: Removing sources of carcinogens in air, water, and food.

Probable Esoteric Psychological Relationship: Anger, self-consumption; a desire to destroy the life force by totally turning away from the "I AM God-Self;" absence of Self-Love. The cosmic fire will not be feeding the kundalini and will be clearly disrupted by the emotions of remorse, fear and internalized anger: deep rooted and long-term issues of the non-tolerant ego not capable of forgiveness. Forgiveness is necessary, but first the person must know what is unforgiven.

Chakra Centers: First, Creative Distributor, third, fourth, fifth and eighth.

Imbalance: Chronic Fatigue Syndrome (see Exhaustion)

Imbalance: Circulatory Disorders (see Arteriosclerosis, Varicose Veins, Heart)

- Symptoms: a reduced flow of arterial and venous blood flow.

Reiki Treatment:

- Treat body and affected area, limbs, etc. Kundalini, heart and adrenals will be weak ,
- *Psycho-Therapeutic Reiki Plus* for the deep emotional conflicts restricting the flow of love.

Nutritional Needs:

- Foods: Eliminate fatty foods, dairy, sugar, caffeine, salt, meats; Introduce fresh juices, vegetables, fruits, nuts, and grains: bananas, broccoli, spinach, beets are needed in diet, eaten raw.
- Herbs: cayenne, garlic and onion; hawthorn berry for heart. Gota kola and Fo-Ti for entire endocrine system.
- Vitamins: B Complex, with additional B6, C, A, E, and timed released niacin, CoQ10.
- Minerals: Multiple, zinc, lecithin granules, chromium, magnesium.
- Special Nutritional/Herbal Combinations: Circulatory Combination, Capsicum Blend, Fiber Blend, Varicose Veins Blend, Grape Seed Pine Bark Combination.
- Homeopathic Tissue Salts: Calc. Flour.

Probable Esoteric Psychological Relationship: A restriction in circulation is holding in love, or the inability (desire) to let it flow to the surface. To contain the fear of being touched or touching; the need to open up the Heart and let love flow through the body. The specific Cardio vascular disorder will describe the psychological pattern of the individuals needs and unresolved challenges of love, be it receiving or giving, and be it to self or others.

Body Parts: Heart, veins, kidneys and arteries.

Chakra Centers: First, third, fourth, and eighth.

Imbalance: Colds, Respiratory

Manifestation: Congestion, tiredness, mucus accumulation.

Reiki Treatment: Full body, lungs, immune and adrenals.

Nutritional Needs: (see Asthma)

- Foods: Eliminate mucous foods. Take citrus juices and beet juices. Fasting to cleanse body.
- Herbs: comfrey, pepsin, fenugreek, peppermint, chamomile, rose hips, golden seal, garlic, lemon balm.
- Vitamins: High potency B-Complex, A (50,000 I.U's or more.), Bioflavonoids (200-600 mg), C (500 mg per hour), B6 (100 mg), E.
- Minerals: Zinc and multiple with trace minerals, and amino acids.
- Special Nutritional/Herbal Combinations: Immune System Combination, Immune Blend, Lung Expectorant Combination.
- Homeopathic Tissue Salts: Kali Mur, Ferrum Phos.

Medical Referral: Physician as symptoms demand.

Probable Esoteric Psychological Relationship: Restriction of the throat center due to repression of inner communication; feeling of too much responsibility compounded upon the individual.

Body Parts: Lungs, throat, adrenals.

Chakra Centers: First, third, fourth, and fifth.

Imbalance: Colitis, Crohn's, Irritable Bowel Syndrome

Manifestation: Mucus or ulceration. Improper digestion of roughage, especially cereals, carbohydrates and mucous-forming foods. Food chewed too quickly, which creates incomplete mastication and saliva, and the consumption of too much fluid at meal time. Can be caused by fluke worms or other parasites.

- Symptoms: Pain, spasm, constipation or diarrhea, flatulence. Hypoglycemia often accompanies these disorders as well as Candida. General inefficient immune system will be present in the Crohn's clients.

Reiki Treatment:

- Full body, additional time on pancreas, adrenals, lower back, colon, and intestines.
- *Psycho-Therapeutic Reiki Plus* necessary to resolve the deep emotions stored in the third chakra. If back problems are also present, then treat with *SAT*sm. Gentle bowel cleansers of an herbal base have

proven effective for suffers of both colitis and Crohn's. Reiki Slaw therapy is equally efficient.

Nutritional Needs:

- Foods: Add Reiki Slaw, carrot juice daily, millet, raw and lightly steamed vegetables, papaya, bananas, and raw cabbage juice. Herbal foods have proven effective in stabilizing the irritable bowels. Digestive enzymes important. Eliminate alcohol, yeast producing foods, acid base diets and caffeine products. Dependent upon the individual's constitution, the tolerance or need of grains, cereals, carbohydrates, mucous-forming foods (dairy products of all types) will vary.
- Herbs: una de gato, lobelia for spasms, aloe, charcoal for bloating, peppermint, fennel or chamomile tea after meals.
- Vitamins: A, C, E High Potency, time released B-Complex, K (alfalfa, parsley, egg yokes); acidophilus capsules from goat's milk and/or goat's yogurt.
- Minerals: Multiple; calcium lactate.
- Special Nutritional/Herbal Combinations: Intestinal Repair Combination, Stress Formula, Stress Combination, Chinese Parasite Cleanse, Chinese Digestive Support Blend, Colon Cleanse Combination, Build Combination.
- Homeopathic Tissue Salts: Mag. Phos. (spasm), Kali Phos. (nerves).

Medical Referral: Nutritionist; Naturopath, Chiropractor, Homeopathic physician, Internist.

Probable Esoteric Psychological Relationship: One's perspective at the whole situation of taking in, processing, and releasing is an aggravation and an irritant. The force of implied or accepted self created imperfection forces the guilt, self-love, insecurity and low self esteem deep into the lining of the colon or intestines, eventually the sense of self worth is so low that the individual begins to ulcerate the pathway of self-nutriment. The acid pH is imbalanced due to this internal fire. This is a Libra disorder, often due to a conflicted positioning of planets at 3-4 degrees Libra in the natal chart.

Body Parts: Colon, throat, stomach, pancreas, adrenals, intestines.

Chakra Centers: Creative Distributor, third, fifth, sixth and seventh.

Imbalance: Constipation/Bowel Congestion (See also: Digestive Disorders)

Manifestation: Peristaltic malfunction in the bowels allowing compaction of fecal matter and difficulty in evacuation of bowels. The improper intake of refined foods, mucous-forming foods, the lack of exercise and stress are contributing factors, as well as inadequate consumption of water, raw vegetables, and potential food allergies.

- Symptoms: Inability to have easy and frequent bowel movements; food in, food out is considered a normal cycle. Normal bowel function consists of two to three effortless bowel movements per day. Constipation can lead to skin disorders including acne, rosacea, psoriasis, and eczema, lung congestion, excessive mucous and catarrh, and sinus congestion and infections.

Reiki Treatment:
- Entire body organs. Additional time on adrenals, lower back, head, and intestines.
- 3 - 7 day fasting with organic raw apple juice, Reiki slaw and water (See chapter 6 on Fasting, *Reiki Plus Natural Healing*). Colonics may be needed.

Nutritional Needs:
- Foods: Water. Digestive Enzymes. Reiki Slaw 1-2 times daily (1 cup total), raw vegetables. Eliminate mucous foods (see Asthma).
- Herbs: cascara sagrada, fenugreek, licorice, aloe vera juice, psyllium seed, Pau D'Arco.
- Vitamins: B-Complex, (B1 - 100 mg), granulated lecithin (3 tbs.), A, E, C, D.
- Minerals: Magnesium
- Special Nutritional/Herbal Combinations: Colon Cleanse Combination, Build Combination, Fiber Blend, Remove Fat Combination, Marshmallow Combination, Chinese Cleanse, Intestinal Flora Blend.
- Homeopathic Tissue Salts: Nat. Mur. (insufficient movement of water in tissue), Calc. Fluor. (strengthens anal and bowel section of colon).

Medical Referral: Nutritionist, Internist.

Environmental changes needed: Exercise such as walking, swimming, jogging, etc.

Probable Esoteric Psychological Relationship: Contained anxiety. Inability to let go of what has willfully been taken into the Mind, Body, Emotions for fear that they will lose it completely. Fearful and possessive personality type. Has a great need for the approval of others. In need of a better sense of self worth. Learn to let go of control and fear.

Body Parts: Adrenals, stomach, intestines, gallbladder, liver.

Chakra Center: Third.

Imbalance: Cyst

Manifestation: A sack of fluid or harden cells, created from various sources of the metabolic congestion, most often due to the lack of proper lymphatic drainage.
- Symptom: A swelling either subcutaneous or inner muscular or in a joint of a limb.

Reiki Treatment:
- Pancreas; Finger point Reiki with the middle finger to direct the energy directly into the cyst.
- *Psycho-Therapeutic Reiki Plus* to reveal the emotions held in the cyst.

Nutritional Needs:
- Vitamins: B6 to help draw fluid from the cyst, A.
- Herbs: una de gato, chamomile, lavender oil applied to the cyst. Consider liver cleanse. Lobelia/Mullein fomentation.
- Special Nutritional/Herbal Combinations: Essiac Tea, Blood Purifying Formula, Detoxification Blend, Dong Quai Combination (ovarian), Special Formula #1. For liver cleanse: Chinese Liver Support Combination.
- Homeopathic Tissue Salts: Silica to drain a subcutaneous soft fluid cyst through the skin internally; Calcium Sulfate to drain a soft cyst internally through the tissue.

Medical Referral: Needed only if discomfort continues and surgical drainage is desired.

Probable Esoteric Psychological Relationship: May be symptomatic of contained emotions correspondence in meaning to the body part where located.

Chakra Center: Fourth and eighth.

Imbalance: Deafness, Hearing Loss

Manifestation: Hearing loss needs medical diagnosis to establish the type of impairment.
- Symptoms: Loss of hearing from allergy or accident (temporal); hearing loss from tumor on fifth cervical nerve (neural) requires medical attention. Ringing in the ears.

Reiki Treatment:
- Ears and inner ear: middle finger at the ear opening and index finger on Eustachian tube drainage point in throat, located by the larynx.
- *Psycho-Therapeutic Reiki Plus*

Nutritional Needs:
- Foods: Allergy: eliminate mucous foods. Fasting in allergy or mucous related hearing losses.
- Herbs: chickweed, ground ivy, sassafras.
- Vitamins: B-Complex.
- Minerals: Manganese, potassium, zinc.
- Special Nutritional/Herbal Combinations: Ear Formula. If hearing loss due to congestion of sinuses and bowels: Colon Cleanse Combination. If due to decreased circulatory function: Circulatory Combination, Butcher's Broom.

- Homeopathic Tissue Salts: Kali Phos. (nerves).

Medical Referral: Hearing specialist to rule out a possible tumor on fifth cervical nerve.

Environmental changes needed: Work conditions which affect the hearing mechanism, loud music, machinery or other sound-producing factors will need eliminating.

Probable Esoteric Psychological Relationship: Shutting down the hearing, not desiring to hear the truth from self or others.

Body Parts: Ears, throat.

Chakra Center: Fourth and fifth.

Imbalance: Depression

Manifestation: The level can range from mild to severe, and there are many types of depression. Depression affects the mind, body, and emotions. Anger, sadness, withdrawal or lack of emotion can all manifest. Heredity may play a role in depression. Depression is a liver disorder in Chinese medicine, and it is considered that depression and anger go hand in hand. Therefore, consider cleansing herbs which support the liver.

- Symptoms: The person feels down, lacks enthusiasm, does not sleep well or sleeps too much, and doesn't feel energized. The loss of life force resulting in a chronic loss of interest in life, ambition and care for self or others.

Reiki Treatment:

- Full body; additional time needed on liver, heart, adrenals and thyroid. Head and coccyx-sacral complex will draw endlessly in extreme cases due to the energy leak in the etheric fabric.
- *Psycho-Therapeutic Reiki Plus* to understand the deeper reasons underlying the depression.
- *PSEB* to align the imbalanced etheric bodies: first, third, fifth, sixth. All may be found with anti-rotational vortices over the chakra center(s), or the entire body will be anti-rotational. Long term depression can lead to external attachment, and/or tears in the etheric bodies. Teach the client to breathe light.

Nutritional Needs:

- Foods: Avoid junk foods. They interfere with neurotransmitters that are responsible for mood. Eat plenty of raw fruits and vegetables, along with complex carbohydrates. Limit wheat intake. Avoid artificial sweeteners and chemicals.
- Herbs: St. John's Wort for mild to moderate depression. Kava Kava, ginger, gingko, ginger, licorice, oat straw, Siberian ginseng, peppermint, mild thistle, evening primrose oil.
- Vitamins: Multiple, with additional B-complex, Vitamin C. Full spectrum amino acids. 5HTP.

- Minerals: Multiple with extra magnesium, zinc. Lithium.
- Special Nutritional/Herbal Combinations: Depression Formula, Energy Combination, 5HTP, Stress Combination, Stress Formula. For monthly PMS concerns: Wild yam, Monthly Support. If thyroid involvement: Thyroid Combination #1 or Thyroid Combination #3. For Liver support: Liver Support Combination, Chinese Liver Support Combination, Liver Support Combination #2, Milk Thistle Blend. Depression Homeopathic Remedy.
- Homeopathic Tissue Salts: Kali Phos, Mag. Phos.

Medical Referral: Holistic Psychologist or Holistic Psychiatrist.

Environmental changes needed: Needs a sun lit environment. Exercise can help relieve depression.

Probable Esoteric Psychological Relationship: The inability to communicate one's needs effectively can lead to depression, as can the feeling of being controlled or trapped by another person or situation. Oftentimes, a person who is depressed has some level of low self-esteem or self-worth, and may not be able to be in touch with any feelings of joy or happiness in life. Not feeling sacred about the use of God's energy and one's own energy; not feeling as if one has a purpose in life. Depression is the inversion of the life force, often due to having too many unlearned lessons of expectations of others to provide for one's needs. This is known as the victim consciousness. Unresolved anger can also lead to muscle and joint pain.

Body Parts: Kundalini disconnection from the clitoris or glans penis, the first chakra, which creates "a hole in the gas tank".

Chakra Center: First, third, fifth, sixth.

Imbalance: Diabetes

Manifestation: Malnutrition and malfunctioning pancreas resulting from overeating refined foods and sugar products, which tends towards an acid metabolism from slowed down digestion of heavy protein foods and fats.

- Symptoms: Improper assimilation of carbohydrates from insufficient insulin production from pancreas. Excessive urinary discharge, thirst and hunger, and emaciation.

Reiki Treatment:

- Full body; additional time needed on pancreas, thyroid, liver, and adrenals. Please note that Reiki has been known to reduce the need of insulin. It is therefore imperative that your client either self check or be checked for the proper amount of insulin. Checks should be at least weekly.
- If the client is using the electrical insulin stimulator, do not Reiki directly over the electrical device.

- High enema of burdock root, yellow dock root or bayberry bark. Physical exercise of utmost importance to stimulate and promote proper oxidation of food.
- Vegetarian diets have proven excellent for food controlled diabetes.
- *Psycho-Therapeutic Reiki Plus*

Nutritional Needs: Eat complex carbohydrates.

- Foods: Raw vegetables, fresh fruits of season. Eliminate meat protein and acid foods, sugars, and caffeine's, refined foods; papaya (digestive enzymes).
- Herbs: nopal, blueberry leaves, blue cohosh, dandelion root, marshmallow root, unicorn, uva ursi. Fo-Ti, Irish moss, bladderwack.
- Vitamins: B-complex, B6 (100 mg) alfalfa (400 mg) and granulated lecithin (3 tbs.) daily have been found effective; kelp (for thyroid); E, A, C.
- Minerals: Potassium, cal-mag; GTF chromium picolinate; selenium.
- Enzymes: Pancreatic.
- Special Nutritional/Herbal Combinations: Pancreas Formula, Ayurvedic Blood Sugar Combination, Pancreas Formula #2, Pancreas Formula #3, Fiber Blend, Circulatory Combination, Grape Seed Pine Bark Combination.
- Homeopathic Tissue Salts: Kali Phos. (Nervous system balance); Natr. Sulp. (excess water in the system); Natr. Mur. (thirst, emaciation).
- Hormones: Adrenal, pancreatic, thyroid, and pituitary.

Medical Referral: Physician, Naturopath.

Environmental changes needed: Eliminate stress factors and food additives.

Probable Esoteric Psychological Relationship: Life is often not sweet enough for the person, no matter how good life is. Psycho-physical desires and feelings of not being nurtured; seeking inner peace to resolve the conflicts of feeling left out and unloved. Nervous system is overloaded and meditation is needed. Throat chakra severely restricted affecting thyroid balance.

Esoteric Anatomical Causal Factor: Balancing adrenals and pancreatic functions - digestive balance to realize that one is being given adequate nurturing for survival.

Body Parts: Adrenals, pancreas, liver.

Chakra Center: Creative Distributor, third, fourth, fifth and eighth.

Imbalance: Diarrhea (See also Digestive Disorders)

Manifestation: Often the body's means of releasing an overloaded system, backed up from a state of congestion and constipation). Allow the body to detox. If excessive or lasting more than 36-72 hours, consult your doctor. Consider a parasitic condition existing in the bowels.

Reiki Treatment: Full body treatments.

Nutritional Needs:

- Allow the body to flush with the aid of water, gently cleansing herbal teas or clear broth vegetable stock soups. Do not fill the digestive system with solid foods unless the body craves them or until it feels ready to accept solid food.
- Vitamins: Potassium
- Herbs: slippery elm, red raspberry liquid, plantago, bayberry.
- Special Nutritional/Herbal Combinations: Intestinal Flora Blend, Bentonite Clay, Activated Charcoal. For suspected parasites: Chinese Parasite Cleanse, Chinese Cleanse, Parasite Homeopathic.

Imbalance: Digestive disorders (See also Constipation, Diarrhea)

Manifestation: Inability to properly digest foods and effect proper assimilation from a variety of metabolic causes: acid-alkaline imbalance; hypertension; diabetes; hypoglycemia, and insecurity.

- Symptoms: Pain in stomach and gastric organs; gas.

Reiki Treatment:

- Full body; digestive organs, thyroid, adrenals, and pancreas will be Imbalanced. Pineal and pituitary will need balancing to establish balance of chakra/gland centers at throat and below.
- Eat slowly and chew foods thoroughly, drink little liquid and combine food types properly - digestive enzymes and hydrochloric production in stomach is capable of manufacturing adequate supply when the stomach is not overloaded or presented foods in the improper order digestion occurs

Nutritional Needs:

- Foods: As noted for type of specific disorders. Do not consume salads or raw vegetables or carbohydrates before eating protein. Food digest in the following order: protein, carbohydrates and vegetables and then fruit. Cultured foods (yogurt, sourdoughs, or sauerkraut are beneficial).
- Herbs: peppermint, anise seed, chamomile flowers, cloves, ginger; wild yams and celery seed prepared as a tea. safflower.
- Special Nutritional/Herbal Combinations: Build combination, Digestive Enzymes, Chinese Digestive Support Blend, Protein Digestion Combination, Intestinal Flora Blend, Colon Cleanse Combination, Stress Combination, Digestive Support Blend, Chinese Cleanse, Fiber Blend, Bowel Combination.
- Minerals: Multi, Magnesium chloride.

- Homeopathic Tissue Salts: Calc. Phos. (digestion); Kali Phos. (gas, nerves); Mag. Phos. (gripping pain - pains with cramps, tight, drawing, lacing sensation as described by Schuessler)

Medical Referral: Naturopath or Nutritionist.

Probable Esoteric Psychological Relationship: Stress and simple overeating or improper mixing and/or consumption of foods. Not taking time to breakdown food (thought-forms) put into one's digestive tract. (See Indigestion). Stress related dysfunction of digestive organs.

Body Parts: Mouth, throat, stomach, pancreas, adrenals, colon, and small intestines.

Chakra Center: Third and fifth.

Imbalance: Edema

Manifestation: Urinary elimination organs not properly functioning (kidneys and bladder) due to lymphatic serum accumulated in the tissue and cells of the body. Inadequate clearing often due to physical inactivity; walking and rebounding are an excellent means for improving lymphatic clearing and drainage.

- Symptoms: Swelling in any part of the body; normally seen in lower limbs when cardio-vascular system has decreased its circulatory efficiency.

Reiki Treatment:

- Body, limbs (elevated to promote drainage if swollen), kidney and bladder.
- Fasting on juice under proper professional supervision (watermelon, pineapple, and cucumber juice). Increase water intake to stimulate kidneys.
- Ginger baths: fresh ground ginger root tied inside cheese or wash cloth (fist size), add 1 tbs. of organic apple cider vinegar for lymphatic cleansing and improved circulation and perspiration. Drink plenty of water during the bath to promote sweating. *If client has high blood pressure, consult client's physician before using hot baths.*

Nutritional Needs:

- Foods: Eliminate meat protein, salt. Increase potassium foods (green leafy vegetables), raw vegetables and fruits and drink 8 - 10 glasses of water daily.
- Herbs: Parsley, dandelion. Lymphatic tinctures.
- Vitamins: A, E, C, B6 (50-100 mg), B-Complex.
- Minerals: Potassium.
- Special Nutritional/Herbal Combinations: Lymph System Support Blend, Lymphostim homeopathic.
- Homeopathic Tissue Salts: Kali Mur (heart, liver or kidneys), Natr. Sulp., Natr. Mur (swelling). Silicea (to open passage ways).

Environmental changes needed: Eliminate stress.

Probable Esoteric Psychological Relationship: Holding on to, within, becoming bloated with retained emotions; (water is correspondent with emotions, the lunar effect).

Imbalance: Emphysema

Manifestation: Reduction of breathing; chronic in nature - mucus contained within lungs; insufficient oxygenation exchange due to inflammation of air sacs.

- Symptoms: Extreme difficulty with exhalation, normally with a wheezing sound of breath.

Reiki Treatment:
30 days of consecutive treatments, with additional healing on thyroid, lungs, and adrenals.

- *Psycho-Therapeutic Reiki Plus* for emotional suppression of restrictive breathing and control issue.
- Fasting to cleanse mucus from body, juice fasting with supplements. Exercise: walking, yoga breathing exercises. Advance cases normally requires the client to sleep sitting up.

Nutritional Needs:

- Foods: Eliminate all mucous foods.; Add raw organic vegetables.
- Herbs: mullein, fenugreek, cayenne, blessed thistle (oxygen carrier).
- Vitamins: A, E (1,000-1,600 I.U.), C (taken 3 or 4 times daily), B-Complex (high potency), B15.
- Minerals: Multiple with trace minerals; amino acids.
- Special Nutritional/Herbal Combinations: Lung Expectorant Combination, Chinese Lung Formula, Respiratory Support Blend, Ayurvedic Lung Formula, Marshmallow & Fenugreek Combination.
- Homeopathic Tissue Salts: Kali Sulp., Kali Mur., Ferrum Phos.

Medical Referral: Respiratory specialist.

Environmental changes needed: No smoking or working in smoke or polluted conditions. Any air pollution aggravates the condition.

Probable Esoteric Psychological Relationship: Extreme closing down of one's will to have the breath of life. Inflamed suppression of emotions. Creative expression and focus is blocked, feeling trapped.

Body Parts: Thyroid, lungs, spleen, pituitary.

Chakra Center: Third, fifth and sixth.

Imbalance: Epilepsy

Manifestation: Loss of consciousness and power of coordination of motion, with convulsions. Symptoms: Convulsions, spasms, unconsciousness.

Reiki Treatment:
- Full body with additional time on head, throat, heart, and adrenals
- *Psycho-Therapeutic Reiki Plus*

Nutritional Needs:
- Foods: Add vegetables, dairy, and grain protein. Juices and fruits (low fructose content best). Eliminate meat, sugar, caffeine, and stimulants.
- Vitamins: B-complex (high potency, timed release), A, C, E, D.
- Minerals: Multiple; especially magnesium, calcium and potassium; zinc.
- Special Nutritional/Herbal Combinations: Lobelia & St. John's Wort with Passion Flower, GABA Combination, Nerve Support Blend, Skeletal Builder, Protein Digestion Combination, Grape Seed Pine Bark Combination.
- Homeopathic Tissue Salts: Kali Mur, Kali Phos., Mag. Phos., Ferrum Phos.

Medical Referral: Neurologist, Nutritionist or holistic physician trained to test for allergies and neurology.

Probable Esoteric Psychological Relationship: Karmic pattern of inwardly contained anger from former lives of violence. Deep seated psycho-physical disorder with neurological and nutritional Imbalances. It is sometimes caused by vicious habits, which drain the vital energy system of nerve minerals.

Body Parts: Neurological system including the brain.

Chakra Center: First and sixth, possibly others.

Imbalance: Exhaustion (Chronic Fatigue Syndrome)

Manifestation: Over expenditure of physical and/or mental reserves; poor nutrition; inadequate motivation of life (the individual is blocking their joy, love, and happiness of and for life experiences) resulting in bio-chemical and hormonal balance; lack of iron and B12, anemia. Any number of disorders can be masked by a lack of energy. Improper oxygenation of foods.
- Symptoms: Tired, depressed, anxious, lack of motivation, impatience.

Reiki Treatment: Full body
- *Psycho-Therapeutic Reiki Plus* for Chronic Fatigue Syndrome for mental and emotional issues.
- *PSEB* to align the imbalanced chakra bodies. Anti-rotational bodies are common, causing massive depletion of physical, emotional, mental and neurological energy that is lost faster than it can be replaced. Usually, the 1st, 3rd, 4th and/or 5th Etheric Bodies are anti-rotational. Exercise is normally lacking due to non-motivation; a gentle and progressive program of yoga, walking, or swimming will benefit the client.

Nutritional Needs:
- Foods: Organic foods - vegetables, fruits, grains and dairy (if not allergic). Some animal and fish protein may be needed to balance if person is alkaline (vegetarian) or suffers from B12 or anemia.
- Herbs: una de gato, morinda, Pau D' Arco, bayberry, yellow dock, gota kola, ginseng (men), dong quai (woman), gingko.
- Vitamins: B-complex (high potency, timed release), A, E, C (throughout the day), D, kelp and high intake of B12 (sublingual or injection from a physician).
- Sources of B12: alfalfa, spirulina, barley, kelp.
- Minerals: Multiple with trace minerals, amino acids, and Zinc.
- Special Nutritional/Herbal Combinations: Thymus Support Combination, Energy Combination, Fatigue/Exhaustion Homeopathic, Chinese Immune Support Combination. B12 Sources: Alfalfa Combination, Spirulina Combination.
- Homeopathic Tissue Salts: Multi of all 12 salts; Kali Phos., Mag. Phos.
- Hormones: May be needed - see your nutritionist or physician.

Medical Referral: Nutritionist. Physician for blood work to check for CMV or Epstein Barr

Environmental changes needed: Stimulating, bright surroundings. Refrain from wearing drab colors; bright hues of red, orange, yellow, pink-rose, gold, and greens are stimulating.

Probable Esoteric Psychological Relationship: Most persons suffering from this disorder are disconnected from their heart. The Creative Distribution of life force from the kundalini is also shut down. This dysfunction needs Etheric Body alignment and deep emotional healing. The resulting dysfunction is related to closing down at the Throat chakra level, to restrict the expression of hurt feelings in the heart, which creates a complex tumbleweed effect on the entire system. If this is Chronic Fatigue Syndrome the individual will display a lack of motivation overshadowed with defensive justifications and with probability of failure built in: the Eyore archetype from *Winnie the Pooh*. Psycho-physically related energy loss needs proper holistic psycho-therapy and nutrition. Achievable goals need to be set. They have achieved a wonderfully self created Victim consciousness and exhibit the Needy Complex.

Body Parts: Kundalini, heart, immune complex and lungs.

Chakra Center: All centers, especially the Creative Distributor.

Imbalance: Eye Disorders

Manifestation: From accident to congenital; diabetic blindness (see Diabetes).
- Symptoms: Poor vision, distortion of vision field, infections.

Reiki Treatment:
- Full body; positions #1 and #3 on head, #4 front (reproduction), and #3 and #4 on back (adrenals)
- *Psycho-Therapeutic Reiki Plus*
- *PSEB* to align the associated chakra body('s) first etheric body for diabetic related blindness; fourth for neurological degeneration or injury.

Nutritional Needs:
- Foods: Vegetables, especially carrots.
- Herbs: eyebright, bilberry, chamomile (soreness), purple losestrife (inflamed or injured), parsley.
- Vitamins: B-complex, A, E, C, D (A from carotene is water soluble; retinol from animal sources is fat soluble). Lutein (a carotenoid).
- Minerals: Multiple.
- Special Nutritional/Herbal Combinations: Eye Formula, Eyebright Combination.
- Homeopathic Tissue Salts: Kali Phos., Mag. Phos. for general. See specific listings in reference.

Medical Referral: Physician, Nutritionist.

Environmental changes needed: Eliminate fluorescent lights, do exercises (Bates method) for improving vision and muscular strength.

Probable Esoteric Psychological Relationship: Visual Imbalances correspond with the psychological perspective of how a person looks and sees life's challenges. I refer you to the course material in *Esoteric Anatomy* for an in-depth explanation of perception. Vision is psychological and can be rebuilt with proper realignment of the psychological perspective.

Chakra Centers: Sixth and second.

Imbalance: Fevers

Manifestation: Infections and/or cleansing toxicity. Fever is the body's way to eliminate foreign host.
- Symptoms: Elevated body temperature above individual's normal temperature. Average human temperature is 98.6 degrees Fahrenheit.

Reiki Treatment:
- Full body, limbs to promote white cell production. Additional time on the immune complex of the thyroid, thymus and spleen, and affected body parts.

Nutritional Needs:
- Foods: Fast with lemon water and juices of vegetables or fruits: carrots or apple (except with ear infections) are good. Eliminate solid foods and especially soft drinks with sugar or chemicals.

- Herbs: red raspberry tea; catnip and wild cherry reduce fever.
- Vitamins: B-complex, A, C (hourly), D, E; B6 and calcium pantothenate (B5). (Vit. C Ascorbate for viral - Ascorbic acid for bacterial.)
- Minerals: Multiple with trace minerals; zinc.
- Special Nutritional/Herbal Combinations: Catnip & Fennel Combination, Chinese Inflammation Combination, Homeopathic Fever Remedy, Parthenium Combination.
- Homeopathic Tissue Salts: Ferrous Phos.

Medical Referral: See appropriate physician if fever persists.

Environmental changes needed: Review nature of illness to stress production for balancing self to environment.

Probable Esoteric Psychological Relationship: Elimination of thought-forms inducing toxicity in the bio-chemistry and cellular functions of the body.

Imbalance: Fibroid Cyst/Tumor

Manifestation: Leiomyoma most often of the uterus - a benign tumor. A fibrous mass of tissue in the reproductive organs.

- Symptoms: Swelling from hard formations in the uterine area.

Reiki Treatment:

- Full body; pituitary, pineal, adrenal, pancreas (proteolytic enzyme stimulation) and reproductive organs, treatments can often continue over several months.
- *Psycho-Therapeutic Reiki Plus* is most beneficial to release contained memories.
- *PSEB* to align the associated chakra body. The 2nd Etheric Body is often anti-rotational, or there is an anti-rotational vortex over the reproductive organs.

Nutritional Needs:

- Foods: Eliminate caffeine, sugars, honey, raisins, meats(they contain synthetic hormones), animal fats and skins, and fried foods. Increase water, papaya, raw juices, fruits and vegetables.
- Herbs: morinda, yellow dock, bayberry, burdock, black walnut.
- Vitamins: B-complex (high potency), A (50,000 I.U.), E (800 I.U., build up 100 I.U. weekly), C (3,000 mg or more of ascorbate). Pancreatic enzymes. CoQ10.
- Minerals: Selenium (150 mcg). Shark cartilage.
- Special Nutritional/Herbal Combinations: Chinese Liver Support Combination, Chinese Blood Support Combination, Liver Support Combination, Enzyme Support Combination, Essiac Tea, Pau D'Arco Program, Red Clover Combination, Special Formula #1,

Detoxification Blend, Chinese Immune Support Combination, Thymus Support Combination.
- Homeopathic Tissue Salts: Calc. Fluor., Kali Phos. (nerves).

Medical Referral: OB/GYN

Environmental changes needed: Needs creative outlet in life.

Probable Esoteric Psychological Relationship: Suppression of sexual needs, guilt and emotions of imbalanced relationship, where anger and fear of loss is most often the dominate factor held within. The client will have unresolved issues with men which will need to be addressed and forgiven. A fibroid is a hardened memory, which has rooted itself into the tissue of the of the uterus. For further insight, refer to book by Christiane Northrup, MD *Women's Bodies, Women's Wisdom.*

Chakra Center: First, second, third and fourth.

Imbalance: Gallstones

Manifestation: Deposits of calcium or cholesterol collected in the gallbladder or duct. Most gallstones are cholesterol and come from excessive carbohydrates and fat intake in the diet. Lecithin is an excellent food to maintain an increased Phospholipid concentration in the bile which breaks down cholesterol.
- Symptoms: Pain in gallbladder; poor digestion of vegetables and fats (animal protein).

Reiki Treatment:
- Full body especially digestive organs & gallbladder. (See *Reiki Plus Natural Healing*, 4th Edition, Chapter 6 on Fasting)

Nutritional Needs:
- Foods: Eliminate soft drinks, sugars, excessive carbohydrates and proteins, salty foods. Increase water and vegetables (green) rich in organic sodium, potassium and magnesium and B-complex foods. Eat apples, pears, prunes, beets, pear juice, apple juice, and applesauce during the Gall Bladder Cleanse.
- Calcium stones: lemon water fast.
- Carbohydrate stones: apple juice. Gall Bladder Flush with olive oil and lemon juice.
- Herbs: hydrangea, parsley, olive oil.
- Vitamins: B-complex, granulated lecithin (500 mg), B6 (extra).
- Minerals: Multiple plus extra magnesium.
- Special Nutritional/Herbal Combinations: Gall Bladder Formula, Fat Digestive Aid, Fiber Blend. If gallbladder has been removed, take Bowel Combination to improve digestion. If Fasting, use Fasting Combination.
- Homeopathic Tissue Salts: Magnesium Phos., Calc. Phos.

Medical Referral: Naturopath, Nutritionist, Physician.

Probable Esoteric Psychological Relationship: A chrysalis attitude and life style. The attitude of the personality internalizes his feelings in a perfunctual and calculated manner, normally incapable of confronting an issue until it seems irreversible and irreparable. The individual might also be found to restrict his creative passions into a rigid mold, becoming a slave to the routine and the diet: restricted fire crystallizes calcium. Caused by the separation of the fourth and eighth chakras due to the conflict of will of the third chakra.

Chakra Center: Third and first.

Imbalance: Headaches

Manifestation: Tension from an imbalance between the seventh and first chakras, and possibly between the fifth and third chakras, leading to blockages in the liver and digestive tracts causing toxicity in the blood, low blood sugar levels and a host of many possible related disorders.

- Symptoms: Pain - acute or chronic - from worry, fear, blood toxicity or nervous anxiety.

Reiki Treatment: Full body

- Position #3 Alternate that balances the blood flow through the carotid artery to the brain and reduces muscular tension in the neck to remove their tightness around the jugular veins, adrenals, liver an intestines. Check reproductive organs, oftentimes involved as the second and sixth chakra imbalance (pituitary and reproductive/creative).
- *Psycho-Therapeutic Reiki Plus* is most beneficial to clear the core memories.
- *PSEB* to align the associated chakra bodies
- Fasting oftentimes needed to eliminate toxicity in body, especially mucus in bowels. Headaches indicate that the proper attention is needed to some specific or multiple associated functions of the body.
- Improper nutrition is oftentimes the underlying culprit.

Nutritional Needs:

- Foods: Eliminate alcohol, sugars, chocolates, milk, caffeine, food additives, cola, flour. Increase raw vegetables, fruits, juices, and water.
- Herbs: feverfew, white willow bark, valerian, chamomile, scullcap, cayenne, gingko.
- Vitamins: B-complex, B6, A, C, D, E, Lecithin granules.
- Minerals: Multiple with trace minerals. Magnesium.
- Special Nutritional/Herbal Combinations: Natural Pain Relief Combination, Homeopathic Pain Remedy, Homeopathic Migraine Remedy. Rub Chinese Essential Oil Blend on temples and back of neck; use Lavender & Peppermint Essential Oils in forehead compress. If headache due to stress: Stress Combination. If due to

liver toxicity: Liver Support Combination. If due to sinus congestion: Sinus Combination, Lung Expectorant Combination.

- Homeopathic Tissue Salts: Kali Phos. (nerves), Ferrum Phos. (inflammation), Kali Mur (sluggish liver), Nat. Mur (not refreshed with sleep, constipation), Mag. Phos. (neuralgic pains-sharp, shooting), Natr. Sulp. (bilious disorders).

Medical Referral: Naturopath, Chiropractic, Neurologist if conditions warrant possibility of tumor.

Probable Esoteric Psychological Relationship: Oftentimes we find the individual can not quit processing the question or turmoil confusing the mind from unresolved conflicts raging between the active/passive and mental/emotional functions of the ego. Then desiring to no longer "think about it," brings on the headache - a way to block out one's ability to confront the issue and accept the truth.

Chakra Centers: Third, fifth.

Imbalance: Headache, Migraine

Manifestation: Triggered normally by stress and anger, which is directly associated with a more complex biochemical Imbalance between the pituitary, adrenal, and reproductive glands (ovaries or prostate/testes). Often begins with puberty or upon the consummation of sexual activity. More prominent in women.

- Symptoms: Blinding pain in the eyes and head normally relieved slightly by lying down in a dark room. Tension held in the ligaments of occiput connected to the condyles, that restrict the flow of blood from the brain through the jugular veins.

Reiki Treatment:

- Full body, head positions#1, #2, #3 alternate, #4; body #1, #2, #4 (ovaries); and back #3/4 (and prostate if male).
- *Psycho-Therapeutic Reiki Plus* for causal factor of the memories associated to this disorder.
- *PSEB* to align the associated chakra bodies.

Nutritional Needs: See Headache.

- Foods: Chocolate, garlic and onions sometimes trigger migraines. Food sensitivity is different in all people.
- Herbs: feverfew.
- Special Nutritional/Herbal Combinations: Natural: Natural Pain Relief Combination, Homeopathic Pain Remedy, Homeopathic Migraine Remedy, Glandular System Blend. Rub Chinese Essential Oil Blend on temples and back of neck; use Lavender & Peppermint Essential Oils in forehead compress. If headache due to stress: Stress Combination. If due to liver toxicity: Liver Support Combination. If due to sinus congestion: Sinus Combination, Lung Expectorant Combination.

Environmental changes needed: Eliminate emotional bondage to social, family, and work influences and expectations.

Probable Esoteric Psychological Relationship: I-Will-Ego struggle is often times present. "I want" is a migraine sufferers key word. Blocked Second Chakra from inability to allow physical freedom always a factor - whether it is induced or imposed. Unconditional Love is not present in the person's life. Sexual trauma and/or guilt are often contributing factors. Will-power and control issues are a trigger in the day-to-day interactions, when unexpressed anger or desired control is internalized. This leads to the eventual sympathetic nervous system response that constricts the blood flow to the brain and causes the ligaments of the cranium to become tense.

Body Parts: Pituitary, thyroid, adrenals, reproductives.

Chakra Center: Sixth, fifth, third and second.

Imbalance: Heart Attack

Manifestation: See Heart Problems

Reiki Treatment: Both hands placed over the heart region: one over and the other below on left side of body.

- Treat for shock: adrenals and/or pituitary if you can not reach adrenals.

Nutritional Needs: Administer no foods or drink.

- Special Nutritional/Herbal Combinations: Chinese Mineral Combination with Capsicum Extract. During recovery: Gingko & Hawthorne Combination, CoQ10, Grape Seed Pine Bark Extract, Bioflavonoids, Vitamin E.

Medical Referral: Immediate medical attention.

Probable Esoteric Psychological Relationship: The heart is the center of all feelings and circulates throughout the entire body the unresolved issues that the individual responded to in a manner that restricted the inflow or out flow of love from the heart. The oxygen molecule is the correspondent to God's breath of Spirit. To restrict the Spirit flowing through the body limits the vital oxygenation to the body. In the case of the heart patient, we find the old adage, "died of heart ache" to be most appropriate in the undeveloped personality. The ache is the selfishly retained and unexpressed grief, pain, remorse, guilt and fear that allows the person to not open himself or herself to the flow of God's love. The human element of love which is temporal still drives the consciousness of many humans. One can only be loved by another equal to the love we accept from God, equated to our parallel acceptance of our Godself and the union of the two of us, our yin and yang, into the trinity: knowing that I am a holy being, unioned through all of my selves with God. No one can give another, what is not first found within the soul's personality.

Chakra Center: Fourth and eighth.

Imbalance: Heart Problems

Manifestation: Physical weakness from birth to extreme emotional build up with the heart. Physically Imbalanced in diet due to high levels of cholesterol triglycerides and fat's in the blood. Lack of physical exercise and poor diet are contributing factors.

- Symptoms: Varying as to type of specific heart disorder.

Reiki Treatment:

- Full body: Position #1 on front, then after gas is released from heart cavity (pericardium sac) treat directly over the heart, *but not until the gas is released*, which may take several treatments. If client has a pace-maker, treat the heart from the back with your hands over the spine at the fourth thoracic vertebra.
- *Psycho-Therapeutic Reiki Plus* is most beneficial to clear painful and unforgiven heart memories.
- *SAT* to release neurological deprivation to the heart.
- *PSEB* to align the associated chakra bodies.

Nutritional Needs:

- Foods: Eliminate refined foods, additives, animal fats, smoking and stress. Add raw vegetables, nuts, grains, and fruits are needed. Lecithin granules break down fat in the body. L-Carnitine.
- Herbs: gingko(unless client is taking beta blockers), hawthorn berry capsules, teas or tinctures, cayenne, Irish moss, garlic, onions, valerian (nerves), licorice (yin quality enhancer), kava kava.
- Vitamins: B-complex, B6, niacin (timed release), A, C (Ascorbate with rutin), D, and E (E should be slowly increased 100 I.U. weekly, up to 1200-1600 mg). CoQ10.
- Minerals: Multiple, with additional magnesium, zinc, chromium, potassium and selenium.
- Special Nutritional/Herbal Combinations: Heart Support Formula, Gingko & Hawthorne Combination, Stress Formula, Chinese Stress Formula, Grape Seed Pine Bark Combination.
- Homeopathic Tissue Salts: Kali Phos. (palpitation and weakness), Ferrum Phos. and Calc. Fluor. (dilation of heart and blood vessels), Kali Mur (embolus), Mag. Phos. and Calc. Phos. (weakness and spasms rebuild muscular strength).

Medical Referral: Cardio-vascular physician; Chiropractor if spinal pain or discomfort is present in between shoulder blades; Nutritionist.

Environmental changes needed: Eliminate stress and smog, and increase exercise to build up heart and circulatory system.

Probable Esoteric Psychological Relationship: Emotions of giving oneself love, and inability to receive or give another love.

Body Parts: Heart.

Chakra Center: Fourth, eighth.

Imbalance: Hemophiliac

Manifestation: A person who has the inability to control bleeding due to a deficiency of coagulation factors.

- Symptoms: A wound or simple cut which will not stop bleeding.

Reiki Treatment:

- Treat wound, and pancreas to stop bleeding. In preventive treatments, full body with additional time on pancreas, spleen, liver, and adrenals.

Nutritional Needs:

- Foods: Sesame seeds and egg yokes (Vitamin T). Soya is a coagulant for the cells of the body and may be beneficial as a protein source in the diet.
- Herbs: cayenne pepper (internal and external); parsley is rich in Vitamin K.
- Vitamins: K, T, and B-complex.
- Minerals: Multiple.

Medical Referral: Immediate medical attention.

Imbalance: Hemorrhoids

Manifestation: Irritation of the anal and sigmoid flexure, resulting in a dilation of a vein of the superior or inferior hemorrhoidal plexus. Insufficient liver function, digestion, and resulting chronic constipation causes varicose veins to swell and protrude within and from the anus.

- Symptoms: Bleeding and pain with difficult bowel movement.

Reiki Treatment:

- Full body; hemorrhoid position with middle finger on anus; liver and digestive tract will need cleansing and treatment.
- Exercise is needed to release stress and to activate bowel movements. If diet is deficient in water consumption, then advise the client that eight to ten 10 oz. glasses of water daily maintains a healthy body.

Nutritional Needs:

- Foods: Eliminate refined foods, mucous foods, sugar, caffeine, and meats. Increase raw or steamed vegetables, sprouts, fruits, grains, and nuts (chewed thoroughly). Papaya and pineapple for digestion.
- Herbs: white oak bark, licorice, burdock, yarrow, golden seal. Consider liver cleanse.
- Vitamins: B-complex - high potency timed release, A, C, D, and E.
- Minerals: Multiple with extra zinc, magnesium and selenium.

- Special Nutritional/Herbal Combinations: Varicose Veins Blend, Chinese Digestive Support Blend, Psyllium Combination, Intestinal Repair Combination.
- Homeopathic Tissue Salts: Natr. Sulp. Kali Mur, Calc. Fluor. (for varicose veins and elastic strength in veins), Mag. Phos. (spasms and cutting pain).

Environmental changes needed: Elimination of stress conditions affecting food cravings leading to poor digestion and constipation.

Probable Esoteric Psychological Relationship: Not willing to process and to let go of your attachments; fear based. Need to learn how to let go of the need to be in control.

Body Parts: Digestive system.

Chakra Center: Second, third.

Imbalance: Hepatitis (See Liver Disorders)

Imbalance: Herpes Zoster (Shingles)

Manifestation: Virus erupting along a nerve path. Highly contagious by contact, most often through sexual contact.

- Symptoms: Open sores, painful.

Reiki Treatment:

- Full body; reproductive area or location of sores.

Nutritional Needs:

- Foods: Eliminate foods with arginine (nuts primarily), refined foods, colas, white flour, chocolate, sugars, and caffeine. Reduce meats and fatty foods. Increase dark leafy vegetables high in potassium, magnesium, and calcium. Foods that cause stress should be eliminated; i.e., drugs and alcohol.
- Herbs: una de gato, Pau D'Arco, burdock, olive leaf extract, and red clover.
- Vitamins: B-complex (timed release, high potency twice daily), A and D, C (throughout day in high dosage recommended). The amino acid L-Lysine is needed to restore Arginine-Lysine balance.
- Minerals: Multiple; magnesium, potassium, and calcium in proper balance; zinc.
- Special Nutritional/Herbal Combinations: Anti-Viral Blend, Homeopathic Viral Remedy, Parthenium Combination, Intestinal Flora Blend,
- Homeopathic Tissue Salts: Natr. Mur, Kali Mur;

Medical Referral: Internist, OB/GYN.

Probable Esoteric Psychological Relationship: If sexual organs are affected, oftentimes it is a result of repressed sexual guilt. The feeling of mot being insulated from the pressures of the world and the body is simply overloaded maintaining the stressful pace.

Imbalance: Hernia

Manifestation: A protrusion of a portion of an organ or tissue through an abnormal opening.

Reiki Treatment:
- Treat the affected area of herniation.

Nutritional Needs:
- Special Nutritional/Herbal Combinations: For Hiatal Hernia, support digestion and stress: Stress Combination, Stress Formula, Catnip & Fennel, Enzyme Support Combination, Papaya Enzyme Blend, Peppermint oil before meals.
- Homeopathic Tissue Salts: Ca . Phos., Ca. Flour., Mag. Phos. & Silica

Imbalance: Hiccups

Manifestation: Spasm of glottis and diaphragm.

Reiki Treatment:
- Place person's hands over his head to stretch diaphragm while you place one hand on the diaphragm and your other hand on the solar plexus.

Nutritional Needs:
- Herbs: peppermint oil or lobelia extract under tongue.
- Minerals: Magnesium deficiency - needs full spectrum of minerals.
- Homeopathic Tissue Salts: Mag. Phos.

Imbalance: Hyperactivity

Manifestation: A disorder normally attributed to children. Adults can be affected also. A variety of learning and behavioral problems which are related may be observed: emotional instability, mood swings, temper tantrums, impatience, poor grades even with above average IQ, self-destructive behaviors, inability to sit for any length of time.

Reiki Treatment:
- Full body. The following areas typically draw a lot of energy: position #2 on the head, position #4 over the throat, and the front and back over the adrenal glands. Teach the child to breathe light up and down the spine to normalize the flow of spinal fluid and the dura membrane rhythm.
- PSEB^sm to align the etheric bodies. Very often you will find anti-rotational etheric bodies, typically first, third and/or fifth.
- *Psycho-Therapeutic Reiki Plus* to calm the child and to bring insight if the child is old enough.

Nutritional Needs:

- Foods: It is extremely important to remove refined and processed sugars and foods, food additives, artificial chemicals, sodas, artificial sweeteners, dyes and colors, and food preservatives. Avoid allergen foods such as milk, wheat, corn, chocolate, and citrus. Avoid red meat and chicken, as these contain hormones and antibiotics. Avoid junk food and fast food. Include whole grains, organic fresh fruits and vegetables, turkey, fish, wheat germ, and organic yogurt and eggs.
- Vitamins: Multiple. B-Complex. GABA.
- Herbs: red raspberry, catnip, valerian, chamomile, hops, lobelia, passionflower, skullcap, thyme wood betony.
- Minerals: Calcium/Magnesium supplement.
- Special Nutritional/Herbal Combinations: Lemon Balm Combination, Valerian Liquid Blend, GABA Formula, Catnip & Fennel, Nerve Support Blend, Stress Formula, Stress Combination, Chinese Stress Formula, Grape Seed Pine Bark Combination, Distress Remedy Homeopathic, Focus Essential Oil Blend.
- Homeopathic Tissue Salts: Kali Phos, Mag Phos, Calc Phos.

Medical Referral: Nutritionist, Cranial-Sacral Therapist, Specialist for ADD. For further information contact Safe Goods at 860-824-5301. They publish a book titled *ADD: The Natural Approach*.

Environmental changes needed: Calming environment with firm but loving boundaries.

Probable Esoteric Psychological Relationship: The belief patterns of the child may be in conflict with his or her environment, thus creating emotional overload and sympathetic nervous system overload. The child or adult may have astral attachments due to emotional and mental patterns.

- Body Parts: Adrenals, digestive, thyroid and immune.
- Chakra Centers: First, third, fifth, with anti-rotations common.

Imbalance: High Blood Pressure (Hypertension)

Manifestation: Improper diet and emotional stabilization leading to any number of associate dysfunction's of organs and glands ultimately affecting the pressure of the blood in the cardio-vascular system. Genetic defects not excluded in the soul's body choice. Due to stress, clogged circulatory system, or kidney/fluid imbalances.

- Symptoms: Red or flushed condition, excess weight and oftentimes pallor of skin. Systolic pressure is too high. Kidney problems are often related to this disorder.

Reiki Treatment:

- Full body and #3 alternate head, adrenal glands and kidneys will require additional time. Note: in cases of very high blood pressure, #3 alternate position should be held with an alternation of the hand on the neck: alternate 10-15 seconds on neck, 10-15 seconds with hand

off the neck. This allows the body to acclimate to the reduction of the blood pressure.
- *Psycho-Therapeutic Reiki Plus* is most beneficial for psycho-emotional, mental and physical imbalance.
- *PSEB* to align the associated chakra body.

Nutritional Needs:
- Foods: Eliminate meat, stimulants, spices (ginger, pepper, mustard, salt, and the like). Increase green leafy vegetables, fruits (not at same meal with vegetables), water and vegetable and/or fruit juices.
- Herbs: cayenne, gingko (unless the client is on beta blockers), garlic, onions, red clover, black cohosh, myrrh, valerian (nerves).
- Vitamins: B-complex - high potency timed release, yeast with GTF chromium, lecithin granules, A, C (Ascorbate), D and E (100 I.U First week, then build 100 I.U. weekly to 400-600 I.U.). Amino Acids.
- Minerals: Multiple, Magnesium.
- Special Nutritional/Herbal Combinations: Circulatory Combination, Capsicum Blend, Garlic Combination, Grape Seed Pine Bark Blend, CoQ10 (100mg capsules), Mineral Combination, Gingko & Hawthorne Combination, Enzyme Support Combination, Papaya Enzyme Blend, Stress Blend, Stress Combination.
- Homeopathic Tissue Salts: Kali Phos., Mag. Phos., Calc. Fluor., Calc. Phos.

Medical Referral: Nutritionist, Internist.

Environmental changes needed: Elimination of stimulus that creates improper diet and conflict in life.

Probable Esoteric Psychological Relationship: Retained anger or conflicts of will power due to unexpressed love affecting the cardio vascular system.

Imbalance: Hypoglycemia (Low Blood Sugar)

Manifestation: This condition is when the body is unable to metabolize carbohydrates normally, reacting to the sugar therein and producing too much insulin to counterbalance.
- Symptoms: Tiredness after eating; craving carbohydrates and sugar foods; depression, anxiety, or other emotional disorders.

Reiki Treatment:
- Full body; pancreas, liver, and adrenals longer.
- *Psycho-Therapeutic Reiki Plus* is most beneficial.
- *PSEB* to align the associated chakra bodies.

Nutritional Needs:
- Foods: Protein from whole grains (uncooked grains digest faster and are not best for this condition), nuts and legumes; limited meat, preferably fish. Raw and steamed vegetables. Eliminate all refined

foods, sugars, caffeine, alcohol and smoking. Juices of fruit should be diluted 50% with water. Eat spirulina in between meals.

- Herbs: juniper berries and licorice.
- Vitamins: B5, B6, B-complex - time release; A, C (several times daily), D and E. Complex amino acids.
- Minerals: Calcium, potassium and magnesium; multiple with trace minerals.
- Special Nutritional/Herbal Combinations: Milk Thistle Blend, Hypoglycemia Blend,
- Homeopathic Tissue Salts: Mag. Phos., Kali Phos., Calc. Phos.

Medical Referral: Nutritionist or physician of internal medicine for proper blood test and allergies.

Environmental changes needed: Elimination of stress.

Probable Esoteric Psychological Relationship: Feeling of not being loved, needing joy in one's life. Needs to reverse emotions to appreciate life's offerings. Sometimes victim consciousness, repressed anger, control issues (irresponsibility), has a tendency to control the love coming in to them (they tell you how they want to be loved).

Body Parts: Pancreas, heart, thyroid.

Chakra Center: Third, fourth, fifth.

Imbalance: Impotence, Male

Manifestation: Lack of sexual copulation.

- Symptoms: Inability to have or maintain erection of penis.

Reiki Treatment:

- Full body; prostate, adrenals, sacral and pituitary.
- *Psycho-Therapeutic Reiki Plus* for emotional blockages.

Nutritional Needs:

- Foods: Your diet should consist of: fruits, vegetables, juices and acidophilus rich foods and capsules, both from goat's milk is best. Buckwheat; millet, sprouted grains and seeds. Eliminate stimulants of caffeine, sugar; salt, refined foods and chemically preserved foods.
- Herbs: garlic, ginseng, gota kola, Fo-Ti, cayenne, kelp, yohimbe, cordyceps, sarsaparilla, damiana
- Vitamins: B6, Lecithin granules, B-complex - high potency, A, C, D, E, RNA tablets.
- Minerals: Zinc, multiple.
- Special Nutritional/Herbal Combinations: Hormone Balancer Formula, Circulatory Combination, Male Action Formula, Masculine Homeopathic Remedy.
- Homeopathic Tissue Salts: Natr. Phos.

Medical Referral: Nutritionist; Urologist.

Environmental changes needed: Look at how one is approaching goal achievement through competitive stress. Is "public" success taking too much energy and eliminating energy for sex. A male's attitude powerfully effects their placement of priority for time and energy allocation. Impotency may be a lack of desire or nonverbal expression, that his needs are no longer being met on a deep emotional level.

Probable Esoteric Psychological Relationship: A fear destroying one's ability to succeed in meeting their own created expectations (role) that they feel their partner must have to unite in a physical bonding. A powerlessness that comes from a "threatened position of insecurity" oftentimes from sexual abuse, guilt, anger or resentment towards one's mother for putting down the male role model in the child's life of the child personally.

Body Parts: Prostate and penis.

Chakra Center: Second.

Imbalance: Indigestion

Manifestation: Improper assimilation and breaking down of foods due to many potential factors: eating wrong food combinations, eating too fast, drinking too much fluid during meals, not chewing food properly and a deficiency of digestive agents (HCL, enzymes, bile, etc.) in the gastro-intestinal system.

- Symptoms: Discomfort after eating, heartburn, gas, diarrhea, constipation.

Reiki Treatment:

- Full body and gastro-intestinal tract, liver, gallbladder, pancreas, and stomach.

Nutritional Needs: (See Digestive Disorders).

- Foods: Examine your current nutritional program.
- Herbs: cayenne (cooked it becomes caustic), garlic, peppermint, pepsin & papaya.
- Vitamins: B-complex, B1, 3, & 6.
- Minerals: Multiple.
- Special Nutritional/Herbal Combinations: Enzyme Support Combination, Papaya Enzyme Blend, Peppermint Oil.
- Homeopathic Tissue Salts: (See digestive disorders.)

Medical Referral: Nutritionist.

Probable Esoteric Psychological Relationship: Long term pattern of feeding self-belief systems that are not digestible. Notice the pattern of the client's food choices and food combinations. They will most often imbalance the acid/alkaline balance of digestion. Food choices often parallel the emotional and mental discourses of the individual.

Imbalance: Infections (see Fevers)

Manifestation: Viral or bacterial. Fungal – See Yeast Infections.
- Symptoms: Elevated temperature; sores with redness, pus, and fevers.

Reiki Treatment:
- Full body; use protective gloves as appropriate if open sores are present.
- Immune complex: thymus-thyroid-spleen; infected area; limbs to stimulate white cell production.
- *PSEB* in affected chakra bodies, increase circulation - especially kundalini and Creative Distributor.

Nutritional Needs:
- Foods: Eliminate sugars, alcohol and caffeine. Increase water with lemon or grapefruit to cleanse liver.
- Herbs: catnip (reduces fever). See specific disorder for correct herbs. Red clover, burdock for liver. Garlic, oregon grape, una de gato, goldenseal, parthenium, echinacea, elderberry.
- Vitamins: B-complex - high potency; B5 supplements; A, D, and E; C hourly (Ascorbate - viral; Ascorbic Acid - bacterial).
- Minerals: Multiple with trace minerals.
- Special Nutritional/Herbal Combinations: Infection Formula, Infection Fighting Combination, Cold Relief Formula, Cold Relief Program, Parthenium Combination, Flu Formula, Elderberry Combination, Children's Elderberry, Colloidal Silver. Homeopathic Remedies: Cold, Fever, Influenza, Viral Recovery, Sinus, Sore Throat/Laryngitis, Prevention. Ear Infection: use Ear Formula.
- Homeopathic Tissue Salts: Ferrum Phos., Kali Mur.

Medical Referral: Seek appropriate medical care.

Imbalance: Infertility

Manifestation: The inability to reproduce biologically due to numerous physiological and hormonal influences.

Reiki Treatment:
- Full body.
- *Psycho-Therapeutic Reiki Plus* is important to find the psycho-emotional, mental and physical causal factor blocking either the receptivity to or giving of life force.
- *PSEB* to align the associated chakra bodies.

Nutritional Needs:
- Herbs: Women: dong quai, damiana, ho shou wu, false unicorn. Men: Korean ginseng.
- Vitamins: Full spectrum B-Complex, E.
- Minerals: Multi mineral. Men: zinc.

- Special Nutritional/Herbal Combinations: Women: Female Corrective, Fertility Formula. Men: Hormone Balancer Formula.

Probable Esoteric Psychological Relationship: If the infertility is not totally physiological: the impossibility to provide the sperm or egg from the reproductive glands or the womb physically incapable of carrying the fertilized egg; then, the causal factor may well be psycho-emotional, mental and physically based. There have been cases where the female is either non-receptive of the sperm or non-giving of the egg due to a variety of emotional reasons and memories.

Imbalance: Insect Stings & Bites (Jellyfish included)

- Symptoms: Swelling, itching. Simple discomfort or possibly anaphylactic shock (allergy reaction of extreme danger closing the windpipe and the ability to breathe, needs antihistamine).

Reiki Treatment:

- At point of bite or sting; treat adrenal's simultaneously to prevent or treat shock. Check Airway, Breathing and Circulation. If necessary administer CPR and if needed Artificial Respiration. If shock or breathing difficulty is present, seek immediate medical attention.
- *PSEB* in affected chakra body and to eliminate the concentration of the protein toxin.

Nutritional Needs:

- Foods: Foods should be withheld until you are sure there is no antigen reaction to the injected protein.
- Herbs: Plantain, tobacco, charcoal, or black tea placed on sting extracts venom. Black Cohosh internally. Lavender oil applied to sting. Pennyroyal oil as insect repellant.
- Special Nutritional/Herbal Combinations: Chinese Essential Oil Blend applied to sting.
- *Alka-selzer Gold* has antihistamines and is effective to treat minor allergic reactions, as is *Benadryl.*
- *Burt's Bees Natural Insect Repellant*

First Aid: For Jelly Fish Stings

- Cleanse the area with ample amount of white vinegar to neutralize the protein. Do not scrap or rub the area, as the nematocysts will release more venomous proteins.
- If you live north of the Chesapeake Bay and from Central to northern Pacific coast area use a mixture of ½ Baking soda to ½ water.
- Apply Benadryl to the surface of the skin to eliminate the stinging and reduce the rash on the skin.

Medical Referral: Emergency medical if required.

Imbalance: Jet Lag

Manifestation: Experienced when traveling from a point west to a point east with five or more hours of time change. Do not retire for the night until the time zone your destination observes.

Reiki Treatment:

- Give yourself a full body treatment several times during flight.
- Epson Salts bath after reaching destination and then retiring at the new bedtime and sleeping until the new locations morning.
- *PSEB* to align the chakra bodies.

Nutritional Needs:

- Foods: Eat only fruits, raw vegetables and other easily digested foods and drink little or no alcohol during flight. Drink plenty of water.
- Herbs: Ginseng for men, Dong Quai for women; Gota Kola and Fo-Ti. Licorice - Pepsin for regularity.
- Vitamins: High potency, timed release B-complex; extra Vit. C; Anti-oxidants for radiation exposure when flying over 28,000 feet.
- Minerals: Multiple, Kelp.
- Homeopathic Tissue Salts: Kali Phos., Mag. Phos., Natr. Mur. Arnica to prevent leg cramps.
- Take Melatonin at night before going to sleep for two nights after reaching destination. This will reset your internal time clock. When you return home, take melatonin for two nights.

Imbalance: Kidney Dysfunctions

Manifestation: Infections or improper and slowed function.

- Symptoms: Pain, infrequent urination, blood in urine.

Reiki Treatment:

- Full body; kidneys, bladder, and thyroid.
- *Psycho-Therapeutic Reiki Plus* for causal imbalance psycho-emotionally.
- *PSEB* to align the associated Chakra bodies

Nutritional Needs:

- Foods: Eliminate caffeine, alcohol, and oxalic acid Foods: cooked spinach, rhubarb, chocolate, cocoa and cola with chocolate. Moderate protein consumption. Increase garlic, potatoes, asparagus and watercress, papaya, bananas, and watermelon. Cranberry juice. Drink 8-10 glasses of spring water daily (with lemon juice if calcium is present in kidneys.)
- Herbs: uva ursi, cranberry, buchu, dandelion, juniper berries, parsley, marshmallow root, and watermelon seeds. Stones: hydrangea.
- Vitamins: B-complex, A, C, D, E. Stones: B6
- Minerals: Multiple. Stones: Magnesium.

- Special Nutritional/Herbal Combinations: Chinese Diuretic Blend, Kidney Blend, Chinese Kidney Support, Kidney Tonic, Cranberry Buchu Formula, Urinary System Tonic, Natural Pain Relief Combo.
- Homeopathic Tissue Salts: Ferrum Phos., Kali Mur., Kali Phos., Calc. Phos.

Medical Referral: Internist, Urologist, Naturopath.

Environmental changes needed: Eliminate social climate of conditional love which restricts the flow of individual's love and joy.

Probable Esoteric Psychological Relationship: Retention of emotions, not knowing if one can release feelings. Highly sensitive person subject to the opinion of others; always desiring to please others and overly seeking to maintain balance. The kidney's purify the blood almost five hundred times a day, and are therefore feeling the emotions of the heart. Impure thought patterns that create discord effect the entire body's harmony. Impure does not mean immoral, but rather critical self judgments based on one's inability to discern reality from illusion (Maya). Fear or rejection of love offered or attracted and/or expressing love

Body Parts: Kidneys and heart.

Chakra Center: Third and fourth.

Imbalance: Liver Disorders

Manifestation: Depression, hepatitis, cirrhosis.

- Symptoms: pain in right upper quadrant of abdomen under ribs, fever, nausea, weakness, joint pain, muscle soreness, drowsiness. With cirrhosis, consider bowel cleansing.

Reiki Treatment:

- Full body; additional time needed on liver, adrenals.
- *Psycho-Therapeutic Reiki Plus*
- *PSEB* paying special attention to first and third bodies.

Nutritional Needs:

- Foods: Avoid sugar, processed foods, alcohol, heavy fats, food additives, chemicals and preservatives. Eat fresh fruits and vegetables, juices, and whole grains. Healthy nuts such as almonds, and include legumes.
- Herbs: milk thistle, olive leaf extract, burdock, red clover, yellow dock, dandelion, aloe vera.
- Vitamins: Multiple with extra B-Complex, C, E. CoQ10, 5HTP.
- Minerals: Multiple with additional calcium and magnesium.
- Special Nutritional/Herbal Combinations: Milk Thistle Blend, Liver Support Combination, Liver Support Combination #2, Chinese Liver Support Combination, Chinese Blood Support Combination, Anti-Viral Blend, Depression Formula. Depression Homeopathic Remedy.

- Homeopathic Tissue Salts: Silicea, Kali Phos, Kali Mur, Ferrum Phos.

Medical Referral: Specialist, Nutritionist, Holistic Psychologist.

Environmental changes needed: Natural, soothing surroundings. Avoid cigarette smoke and alcohol. Mild exercise.

Probable Esoteric Psychological Relationship: The liver relates to one's passions in life. Internalization of fire energy, the ego turned inward. The inability of the ego to surrender to the heart and listen to the Higher Self.

Body Parts: Liver, adrenals, heart, thyroid.

Chakra Center: First, third, fourth, fifth, eighth.

Imbalance: Memory Loss, Impairment

Manifestation: Stroke; nutritional deficiency; mental exhaustion; neurological breakdown in brain passageways.

Reiki Treatment:
- Full body; position #2 head and adrenals.
- *PSEB* to align the imbalanced chakra bodies.

Nutritional Needs:
- Foods: Increase "alive foods" - fresh fruits, vegetables and juices. Nuts, grains, and legumes. Soya foods. Eliminate fatty meats, fried refined foods, alcohol, tobacco, and caffeine.
- Herbs: cayenne, gota kola, Fo-Ti, gingko, suma.
- Vitamins: B-complex, B1, B3 (niacin - timed release), and B6. Lecithin granules. Amino acids, especially L-Glutamine; A, C, D, and E. CoQ10.
- Minerals: Multiple; potassium, chromium, zinc, manganese, selenium.
- Special Nutritional/Herbal Combinations: Brain Formula, Circulatory Combination, Mineral Combination, Grape Seed Pine Bark Combination, Gingko, Gotu Kola Combination.
- Homeopathic Tissue Salts: Calc. Phos, Kali Phos.

Medical Referral: Nutritionist, Neurologist

Imbalance: Menopause – see Menstrual Disorders

Imbalance: Menstrual Disorders

Manifestation: Any number of physical, hormonal and emotional causes; however, all three factors are normally found present in all disorders.
- Symptoms: Various - pain, scanty flow, excessive flow, irregular cycle, lower back pain, cramps, mood swings.

Reiki Treatment:

- Full body; pineal, pituitary, thyroid, adrenals, and reproductive organs.
- *Psycho-Therapeutic Reiki Plus* for psycho- emotional trauma from abortions, abuse.
- *SAT* for psycho-physical & emotional with sacral or lower lumbar subluxation.
- *PSEB* to align the associated chakra bodies

Nutritional Needs:

- Foods: Decrease excessive meats. Protein from more natural organic sources. Eliminate caffeine, sugar, chocolate, alcohol, and refined carbohydrates. Include soy foods.
- Herbs: dong quai, yarrow, uva ursi, red raspberry, wild yam, squaw vine, blue or black cohosh (scant menses - promotes discharge of wall lining). Black or blue cohosh - do not use if pregnancy is suspected because it can promote uterine contractions, possible abortion or miscarriage. Sarsaparilla, Evening Primrose Oil
- Vitamins: B-complex; B6. DHEA.
- Minerals: Multiple; calcium, magnesium, and potassium.
- Special Nutritional/Herbal Combinations: Monthly Support, Energy Combination, Female Corrective, Female Corrective #2, Female Corrective #3, Female Corrective #4, Progesterone Cream, Female Changes Program, Soy Capsules, Hot Flash Relief Formula. Homeopathic Remedies: PMS, Menstrual, Menopause, Feminine Tonic.
- Homeopathic Tissue Salts: Kali Phos., Mag. Phos., Calc. Phos.

Medical Referral: OB/GYN; Nutritionist; Chiropractor if lower back pain is not relieved.

Probable Esoteric Psychological Relationship: Oftentimes relates to sexual suppression, guilt or emotional fears due to unexplained phenomenon or normal womanhood. Abortions, even when mentally justified, always leave emotional trauma with strong potential to manifest abnormal cellular function, such as cyst on the ovary(s). For further insight, refer to book by Christiane Northrup, MD *Women's Bodies, Women's Wisdom.*

Chakra Center: Second, sixth.

Imbalance: Mental Illness

Manifestation: Multiple classifications of psychosis. Acid balance metabolism needs nutritional balancing.

- Symptoms: Dependent upon psychosis. Basic disability to function normally under everyday life stresses.

Reiki Treatment:

- *Psycho-Therapeutic Reiki Plus* treatments may be possible to unlock collective unconscious and soul memory that has led to the psycho-mental disorder.
- *PSEB* to align the associated chakra bodies

Nutritional Needs:

  - Variant - dependent upon nature of psycho-physical disorder, proper nutrition essential.
- Foods: Eliminate sugars, refined foods, chocolates, and "empty foods."
- Herbs: Fo-Ti, valerian, kelp, gota kola, ginseng (men).
- Vitamins: B-complex plus specific concentrates dependent upon psychosis; C, A, D, and E are needed as anti-oxidants. L-Glutamine amino acid.
- Minerals: Multiple plus specific minerals; magnesium, zinc and calcium.
- Special Nutritional/Herbal Combinations: Depression Formula, Brain Formula, Herbal Tranquilizer Blend, Nerve Support Blend, Stress Combination, Hops Combination.
- Homeopathic Tissue Salts: Kali Phos., Calc. Phos., Ferrum Phos., Natr. Mur., Mag. Phos., Natr. Sulp.

Medical Referral: Psychologist, Nutritionist

Environmental changes needed: Stressful environment changed and individual's attitude adjusted in response to stress-related stimuli.

Probable Esoteric Psychological Relationship: Psycho-physical imbalances are deeply rooted emotional manifestations which affect the behavior of the individual and incapacitates normal activity.

Chakra Center: All chakras, especially third and sixth.

Imbalance: Motion Sickness

Manifestation: Can be either gallbladder or middle ear related. Acid foods eaten on an empty stomach can cause nausea under rough or curvy road or traveling conditions, i.e. rocking boat in wave swell.

- Symptoms: Nausea, dizziness, loss of balance (vertigo).

Reiki Treatment:

- Full body; ears, Eustachian tubes (under jaw), and gallbladder.

Nutritional Needs:

- Foods: Avoid rich and acid foods that are hard to digest.
- Fasting to cleanse gallbladder is advisable.
- Herbs: Ginger, papaya, cayenne for digestion and mucus, charcoal. Take ginger every two to three hours before traveling.
- Vitamins: B1 and B6 (best taken before traveling).
- Minerals: Multiple, magnesium.

- Special Nutritional/Herbal Combinations: Papaya Enzyme Blend, Flu Formula (for nausea).
- Homeopathic Tissue Salts: Ferrum Phos.

Probable Esoteric Psychological Relationship: Anxiety or fear of being uprooted from security or home. The individual needs stability in their life. Psycho-emotional or mental trauma unconsciously associated with travel.

Body Parts: Gallbladder, solar plexus; ears and Eustachian tubes.

Chakra Center: Third, fifth (if ears).

Imbalance: Mumps

Manifestation: An acute, contagious viral disease, involving salivary glands, parotids, and other tissues such as the meninges, testes, ovaries, or pancreas.

- Symptoms: Swelling under jaws in children. Adult males who contract mumps can have severe difficulty from the swelling of their testes.

Reiki Treatment:

- Children: Treat after second symptomatic day: allows immune system to develop immunity.
- Adult Male: treat immediately if never exposed to mumps; treat testes.

Nutritional Needs: See Infections.

- Herbs: Lobelia (1 part) and Mullein (3 parts) – make tea and soak cotton cloth. Wrap around neck and cover with plastic. Change every hour the client is awake.
- Special Nutritional/Herbal Combinations: Anti-viral Blend, Thymus Support Combination, Infection Formula, Natural Pain Relief Combination, Immune System Combination, Immune Blend, Lymph System Support Blend, Parthenium Combination, Infection Fighting Formula. Homeopathic Remedies: Viral Recovery, Fever, Pain, Lymph Stimulant.
- Homeopathic Tissue Salts: Ferrum Phos. (fever), Kali Mur., Natr. Mur. (swelling of testicles).

Medical Referral: Seek medical attention.

Imbalance: Multiple Sclerosis

Manifestation: Loss of myelin sheath (coating protecting nerve shaft in the brain or spinal column) throughout the white matter of the central nervous system, sometimes extending into the gray matter. Lesions result.

- Symptoms: Weakness, uncoordinated, speech disturbances, visual complaints, burning, prickling sensation.

Reiki Treatment:
- Full body; liver, pancreas and adrenals; pituitary, pineal and thymus will be severely blocked.
- *PSEB* to align the associated Chakra bodies

Nutritional Needs:
- Foods: Eliminate alcohol, sugar, chocolate, caffeine, refined foods, mucous forming foods, preservatives, chemicals, processed foods. Increase green leafy vegetables, fruits, juices. Use molasses and honey as sweeteners in limited quantities or stevia. Avoid wheat, oats, barley, spelt or rye unless sprouted. Raw sprouted seeds. Drink fresh vegetable juices and lemon in water. 1/3 cup chlorophyll plus one egg yolk to feed the myelin sheath.
- Herbs: Evening primrose, sarsaparilla, black walnut.
- Vitamins: B1, B3, B6, B-complex, E, F, C, granulated lecithin, Brewer's Yeast.
- Minerals: Potassium, magnesium, germanium, multiple.
- Special Nutritional/Herbal Combinations: Grape Seed Pine Bark Combination, Immune Blend, Thymus Support Combination, Germanium Blend, Nerve Support Blend, Digestive Enzymes, Herbal Calcium Blend, Skeletal Builder, Mineral Combination. Cleanse body and bowels with Colon Cleanse Combination and Detoxification Blend. Feed the Nerves and reduce Stress.
- Homeopathic Tissue Salts: Natr. Phos.

Medical Referral: Nutritionist, Internal Medicine Allergists have found food sensitivity to be a major factor related in MS.

Probable Esoteric Psychological Relationship: Hardened attitude, unchangeable resistance to filtering emotions. Behavioral needs oftentimes leads to taking in "passion" oriented drinks and drugs to block out unexpressed emotions. Need to provide creative outlet on physical plane to regain loss of power and sense of life-giving purpose. Needs to be in control; spiritual values and selfishness need up-lifting to selfless values.

Body Parts: Liver.

Chakra Center: Third, fourth, sixth, eighth.

Imbalance: Nerve Problems

Manifestation: An inflammation of the nerves from any number of causal factors. Normally considered as a primary or secondary physiological disorder as related to the type of disorder within the framework of a psycho-physical disease.
- Symptoms: Fatigue, spasms, hypertension, heart palpitations, high blood pressure, insomnia, memory loss, muscle cramps, fear, anxiety, paranoia and many other psycho-physical disorders.

Reiki Treatment: Full body; extra time over chakras.

- *SAT* to clear any spinal imbalance and psycho - emotional, physical and mental interferences.

Nutritional Needs:

- Foods: Eliminate caffeine, salt, sugars, drugs, alcohol, refined foods, food additives, and allergen agents. Increase green leafy vegetables, granulated lecithin and easily digested foods. Reduce heavy meats, dairy, carbohydrates.
- Herbs: Chamomile, kava kava, damiana leaves, Irish Moss, licorice, valerian., Gingko, St. John's wort, passion flower, hops, catnip.
- Vitamins: B-complex - timed release, high potency; B6, B3, folic acid, pantothenic acid (B5) and A, C (large amounts throughout day), D and E. Amino acids.
- Minerals: Multiple; trace minerals. Potassium-calcium-magnesium.
- Special Nutritional/Herbal Combinations: Stress Combination, Stress Formula, Energy Combination, Nerve Support Blend, Nerve Combination, Chinese Stress Combination, Fatigue/Exhaustion and/or Nervousness Homeopathic Remedy.
- Homeopathic Tissue Salts: Kali Phos., Kali Mur., Kali Sulp. (skin), Calc. Phos., Mag. Phos. (spasms).

Medical Referral: Physician, Nutritionist, Chiropractor if spinal deformation is present.

Environmental changes needed: Attitude of client to environmental agents necessary. Pollution, foods, and chemicals need identifying which might act as allergens to upset neurological balance.

Probable Esoteric Psychological Relationship: This disorder will be correspondent to the specific body function(s) that are affected by nervous system Imbalance. Overall Imbalance to stress from fear center. Meditation with cosmic fire visualization is an important ingredient in the healing.

Body Parts: Adrenals, pineal, pituitary, hypothalamus, left-right hemisphere balance and central nervous system.

Chakra Center: First, sixth, eighth.

Imbalance: Nose Bleed

Manifestation: Rupturing of capillary vessels within mucous membrane lining of nose.

- Symptoms: Bleeding from nose.

Reiki Treatment:

- Position head at a 45 degree angle forward. Place ice pack on the occipital lobe (head #3) and Reiki the nose. Have client place index fingertips on pressure points located at center of cheekbones. Reiki pancreas to produce platelets.

Nutritional Needs:
- Herbs: Cayenne, parsley. Sniff goldenseal powder. Chlorophyll.
- Vitamins: B-complex, A, E, C, D, K, Bioflavonoids.
- Minerals: Multiple with trace minerals.
- Homeopathic Tissue Salts: Ferrum Phos., Kali Phos. (for easy-bleeder), Natr. Mur. (anemic).

Medical Referral: If bleeding does not cease in a reasonable time period, seek medical assistance.

Imbalance: Parkinson's Disease

Manifestation: Neurological disorder with marked abnormally diminished motor activity (hypokinesia), tremors and muscular rigidity. An unknown caused degeneration of tissue around the thalamus gland and midbrain tissue matter. Oftentimes a sequel of epidemic (lethargic) encephalitis (inflammation of the brain).
- Symptoms: Tremors, progressive degeneration of the nerves and muscles.

Reiki Treatment:
- Full body; limbs, thymus, spleen, liver and pituitary (all head positions).
- *SAT* will best treat neurological disorders of the central nervous system.
- *PSEB* to align the neurological body.
- Mental - emotional energy for gentle balancing and internal neurological balancing.

Nutritional Needs:
- Foods: 100% raw food diet of organically grown foods with low protein structure. Raw seeds, nuts & grains, sprouts, raw milk, raw fruits and vegetables, green leafy vegetables, rutabaga—pure gelatin.
- Herbs: gingko, valerian, chamomile, ginseng, cayenne, damiana, scullcap, gotu kola, Pau D'Arco.
- Vitamins: Granulated Lecithin, B-complex, B12, L-Glutamine. Low intake of B6 for amino acid functions.
- Minerals: Multiple, calcium, magnesium, manganese, potassium, trace minerals.
- Special Nutritional/Herbal Combinations: Brain Formula, Stress Formula, Chinese Stress Formula (feed nerves), Stress Combination, Food Enzyme, Circulatory Combination, Mineral Combination, Grape Seed Pine Bark Combination.
- Homeopathic Tissue Salts: Mag. Phos. (muscles), Calc. Phos. (nerves), Kali Phos. (nerves and muscles).

Medical Referral: Nutritionist for proper administration of amino acids L-dopa, tyrosine and phenylalanine. Medical attention should be sought; Neurologist.

Environmental changes needed: Elimination of airborne and food-born chemicals.

Probable Esoteric Psychological Relationship: The degeneration of neurological, muscular functions is a withdrawal process; stemming from contained anger representing nondirected creativity to achieve ones own goals: suppression and non fulfillment. Has a control issue. The individual's perceptual evaluation of his or her innate capabilities has been out of focus.

Chakra Center: First, third, sixth.

Imbalance: Plantar Wart

Manifestation: An epidermal tumor of viral origin on the sole of the feet.
- Symptoms: Formation of wart on the sole of feet, oftentimes with a granular surface, formed by more than one wart.

Reiki Treatment:
- Soak foot for 30 minutes daily to soften, apply Vitamin E oil and then treat foot and full body. Apply gauze bandage over wart. Green papaya juice on wart has been found to help.

Nutritional Needs:
- Foods: Figs, asparagus.
- Herbs: Sassafras (apply syrup mixture to wart), Pau D'Arco, tea tree oil.
- Vitamins: E, A, B-complex.
- Special Nutritional/Herbal Combinations: Blood Purifying Formula, Anti-Viral Blend, Colloidal Silver, Pau D'Arco Lotion, Chinese Essential Oil Blend. Viral Homeopathic Remedy.
- Homeopathic Tissue Salts: Kali Mur.

Medical Referral: Podiatrist

Probable Esoteric Psychological Relationship: Location on which foot might provide a link to other psycho-physical stress manifesting in the individual. The reflexology chart should be consulted to find corresponding body part and glands.

Imbalance: Pneumonia

Manifestation: Inflammation of the lungs from foreign matter or bacteria resulting in congestion, mucus and fluids contained within the lobes. Biochemic medicine considers that weather (cold) and electrical atmospheric changes. Imbalance the levels of Kali Mur (potassium chloride) and Ferrum Phos. (iron), which produces an excess release of fibrin which eventually clog the mucus membranes of the lungs. Pneumonia results from this produced weakness and creates a breeding ground for bacteria.

- Symptoms: Congestion of lungs, wheezing, inability to achieve satisfying breath, coughing, yellow-green exudation.

Reiki Treatment:

- Full body; thyroid, pituitary, thymus, spleen, liver and lungs will require extensive treating.
- Treat limbs and joints for pain from fever and to stimulate white cell production.
- Treatments given daily until lungs are clear.
- Never turn a pneumonia victim on his stomach, treat back of lungs by placing hands behind back.
- Prop person up to approximately a 30 degree angel to keep mucus in lower lung region away from the bronchial tubes.
- Treatment time can be as long as 2 - 3 hours in the beginning.
- Group treatment and assistance through Absentia beneficial.

Nutritional Needs: (See Infection, Inflammation, Asthma).

- Foods: Fruit and vegetable juices; eliminate from diet sugar food, chocolate, caffeine, and alcohol.
- Herbs: Mullein, lobelia, and cayenne for mucus. Ginseng for adrenal stimulation. Una de gato.
- Vitamins: B-complex (timed release, high potency twice daily), A, E, D, and C (1,000 mg. hourly for fever and infection -- ascorbic for bacterial and ascorbate for viral); B6 and Calcium Pantothenate.
- Minerals: Multiple; Zinc, germanium.
- Special Nutritional/Herbal Combinations: Chinese Lung Formula, Lung Expectorant Combination, Anti-Viral Blend for viral pneumonia, Intestinal Flora Blend, Respiratory Support Blend, Infection Fighting Formula, Grape Seed Pine Bark Combination.
- Hormones: Thymus, spleen, adrenal, and thyroid; maybe pituitary.
- Homeopathic Tissue Salts: Ferrum Phos. (first stage), Kali Mur. (second stage), Calc. Sulp. (last stage), Natr. Mur. (watery, frothy expectoration), Kali Sulp. (yellow, slimy expectoration).

Medical Referral: Seek medical attention for proper treatment and diagnosis.

Probable Esoteric Psychological Relationship: Attitude of being suffocated without ability to fight back or change conditions; drowning in contained emotions: repressed and limited life force. Desire to communicate is blocked or they feel it would be useless.

Body Parts: Respiratory.

Chakra Center: Third, fourth, fifth.

Pregnancy (all trimesters)

Manifestation: The conscious decision of the incoming soul for the fertilization of the selected mother through chosen father.

- Symptoms: Elimination of menstrual cycle, morning sickness, progressive enlargement of uterus.

Reiki Treatment:

- Excellent for a mother to Reiki her child throughout the pregnancy: this creates a loving and bonding atmosphere of exchange. Treatment every day, starting several weeks prior to delivery allows an easier delivery. Especially relaxing for pain and tension during contractions.
- *Psycho-Therapeutic Reiki Plus* if any emotional conflicts are effecting the carriage of the fetus.

Nutritional Needs:

- Foods: Eliminate alcohol, refined foods, sugars, sugar substitutes, ice creams, smoking (primary and secondary smoke inhalation), fats and "empty foods." Include fresh fruits, vegetables (especially dark green leafy ones). Use stevia as sweetener.
- Herbs: Red raspberry tea will tone uterus and ease labor pains. Wild yam, chamomile, ginger, burdock, lobelia, yellow dock.
- Avoid these herbs: golden seal, wormwood, barberry, oregon grape, angelica, coffee, eucalyptus oil, juniper, lovage, ephedra, mistletoe, mugwort, pennyroyal, poke root, rue, shepherds purse, tansy, yarrow.
- Vitamins: A, B-complex, C, E, Folic acid.
- Minerals: Multiple chelated, rich in calcium.
- Special Nutritional/Herbal Combinations: Prenatal Combination, Folic Acid Combination, Alfalfa Combination, Skeletal Builder, Fiber Blend, Female Corrective #4 in last five weeks. To adjust hormones: Dong Quai Combination, Female Corrective #2, Progesterone Cream, Red Raspberry. To prevent morning sickness, clean the liver: Liver Support Combination, Liver Support Combination #2, Chinese Liver Support Combination (for stressed condition), Chinese Blood Support Combination (for weakened condition). To treat morning sickness: ginger, Papaya Enzyme Blend, peppermint oil, red raspberry, Digestive Support Blend. Women with severe nausea may be infected with the Heliobacter pylori bacteria, which causes ulcers, therefore use the HP herbal fighter combination. For hemorrhoids/Varicose Veins: Varicose Veins Blend, White Oak Bark, Butcher's Broom.
- Homeopathic Tissue Salts: Kali Phos. (entire pregnancy); Mag. Phos. (labor pains); Ferrum Phos. (after labor or miscarriage) then Calc. Fluor. and Calc. Phos.; Natr. Mur. (morning sickness).

Medical Referral: OB/GYN.

Imbalance: Prostate Disorder

Manifestation: Inflammation of prostate gland.

- Symptoms: Pain in prostate due to enlargement of gland.

Reiki Treatment:
Full body; pituitary and prostate. Regular sexual intercourse may help to eliminate build-up of prostate fluid.
- *Psycho-Therapeutic Reiki Plus* to release contained resentments.
- *PSEB* to align the appropriate Chakra bodies

Nutritional Needs:
- Foods: Eliminate caffeine. Bee Pollen should be added to diet.
- Herbs: saw palmetto, burdock, ginseng, true unicorn, kelp.
- Vitamins: F, granulated Lecithin (4 tbsp. daily), E, C, B6; B-complex.
- Minerals: Zinc; Multiple.
- Special Nutritional/Herbal Combinations: Male Formula, Prostate Blend #1, Prostate Blend #2, Progesterone Cream Combination, Soy Capsules. Keep bowels clean with Colon Cleanse Combination and Chinese Parasite Cleanse. To kill parasites and provide zinc use Pumpkin Blend.
- Homeopathic Tissue Salts: Ferrum Phos., Calc. Sulp. (suppurating abscess in gland).

Medical Referral: Urologist.

Environmental changes needed: Prolonged sitting, squatting and lifting which places strain on weakened abdominal muscles; exercises to strengthen lower bladder and anterior muscles of anus. Utilize sitz baths.

Probable Esoteric Psychological Relationship: Feeling incomplete in divine spiritual-sexual connection with mate or partner: seeking gratification while a disconnection of heart and physical union exist from fear of not being loved by the mate. Potential rejection of women due to the male's relationship to his mother.

Body Parts: Reproductive.

Chakra Center: Second, sixth.

Imbalance: Pyorrhea (Gum Disease)

Manifestation: Discharge of pus from gums.
- Symptoms: Pus and bleeding from gums.

Reiki Treatment:
- Full body, gums for 20-30 minutes; with tissue on gums, press gently to release pus collected under gums. Have client rinse with warm sea salt water and treat for another 20-30 minutes to strengthen gums. Repeat process during follow-up treatments next two days.

Nutritional Needs: See Infections/Inflammation
- Food:: Fish, poultry, meat, whole grains, eggs, nuts, seeds.
- Herbs: cayenne, golden seal, bayberry, una de gato, white oak bark, tea tree oil.

- Vitamins: A, D, B-complex, C, Bioflavonoids, E. CoQ10.
- Minerals: Phosphorus, (calc., magnesium and potassium for proper balance) maybe too much magnesium off-setting phosphorus in diet.
- Special Nutritional/Herbal Combinations: Grape Seed Pine Bark Combination.
- Homeopathic Tissue Salts: Kali Phos., Calc. Fluor, Ferrum Phos.

Medical Referral: Holistic Dentist; Nutritionist.

Environmental changes needed: Often results from smoking pipe, poor oral hygiene.

Probable Esoteric Psychological Relationship: Inflammation from chewing improperly for too long with an attitude of ridge and stoic; holding on to, rather than digesting, letting go.

Body Parts: Throat, ears.

Chakra Center: Third, Fourth and Fifth

Imbalance: Rheumatism - See Arthritis

Manifestation: Any of a variety of disorders marked by inflammation, degeneration, or metabolic derangement of the connective tissue structures, especially the joints and related structures.

- Symptoms: Pain, limitation of motion and stiffness.

Reiki Treatment:

- Treat afflicted areas; full body.
- If located in the spinal then treat with *SAT* or polarity running Reiki energy.
- *Psycho-Therapeutic Reiki Plus* for understanding emotions underlying the chronic disorder.
- *PSEB* to align the associated Chakra bodies

Nutritional Needs: (See Arthritis)

- Special Nutritional/Herbal Combinations: Antioxidant Combination, Grape Seed Pine Bark Combination, Yucca, Joint & Structural Combination, MSM Combination Cream.

Imbalance: Sciatica

Manifestation: Inflammation of sciatic nerve from organic or inorganic caused Imbalance of lumbar vertebra and/or sacral-pelvic bones. Fourth lumbar subluxation causing neurological interference.

- Symptoms: Pain or discomfort down one leg, radiating from lumbar-sacral region in the pelvis. Can appear localized at any or multiple areas of the hip down to the foot.

Reiki Treatment:

- Full body. Sacral and entire sciatic nerve of both legs.
- *SAT* to treat spinal column.

- *Psycho-Therapeutic Reiki Plus*
- *PSEB* to align the associated chakra bodies

Nutritional Needs:
- Foods: Eliminate caffeine, salt, sugars, drugs, alcohol, refined foods, and allergen agents. Add green leafy vegetables, granulated Lecithin, and easily digested foods. Reduce heavy meats, dairy, carbohydrates.
- Herbs: chamomile, damiana leaves, Irish moss, licorice, valerian.
- Vitamins: B-complex, folic acid, pantothenic acid, and A, C, D, and E; amino acids.
- Minerals: Calcium, magnesium, and potassium.
- Special Nutritional/Herbal Combinations: Joint & Structural Combination, MSM Combination Cream, Morinda, Chinese Inflammation Combination, Natural Pain Relief Combination, Chinese Bone Support, Skeletal Builder, Herbal Calcium Blend, Shark Cartilage. Homeopathic remedies: Sciatica, Pain.
- Homeopathic Tissue Salts: Kali Phos., Mag. Phos. (pains), Natr. Sulp. (gout), Ferrum Phos. (fever), also Calc. Phos.

Medical Referral: DNFT or Network Chiropractor.

Probable Esoteric Psychological Relationship: Clarity of one's motivation of "pride" to withstand constrictive burdens by not admitting Imbalanced sense of traditional-normative-social and religious values in molding one's accepted role of responsibility. Oftentimes it is a sexual or creative energy blockage affecting the lumbar and sacral balance.

Body Parts: Spinal.

Chakra Center: First, second, third.

Imbalance: Scoliosis of the Spine

Manifestation: Spinal degeneration/discomfort from lateral movement.
- Symptoms: Spine has an "S" or "C" curvature: lateral, posterior and anterior. Imbalanced posture, pain and discomfort from sitting too long in one position.

Reiki Treatment:
- Full body; full treatment down each side of the spine, complete with spinal polarity.
- Yoga and gentle stretching with exercises to strengthen spine very important.
- *SAT* or run Reiki through spine using polarity hand placements - see *Reiki Plus Natural Healing*, Chapter 7.
- *Psycho-Therapeutic Reiki Plus* for understanding the emotions underlying the chronic disorder.
- *PSEB* to align the associated Chakra bodies

Nutritional Needs:
- Foods: Eliminate mucous-forming foods, refined sugars, flours and processed and preserved foods. Reduce caffeine and eliminate alcohol. Eat green leafy vegetables, nuts and grains.
- Herbs: Irish moss.
- Vitamins: B-complex.
- Minerals: Magnesium, calcium, manganese, chromium, zinc.
- Special Nutritional/Herbal Combinations: Joint & Structural Combination, Chinese Bone Support, Skeletal Builder, Herbal Calcium Blend.
- Homeopathic Tissue Salts: Calc. Phos.

Medical Referral: Chiropractor.

Probable Esoteric Psychological Relationship: Disproportionate distribution of stress. Body parts, organs, and chakras will be represented by the specific point or points where the "S" curvature is fixated in the individual vertebra. Clarity of focus and life's goals are needed. Yin-Yang quality and attitude will be noticeable by studying the directions of the curvature; and, the needed alteration of personality and perspective can be delineated from this subtle map. Many past life issues carried into this incarnation by the soul to challenge its growth.

Chakra Center: Noted by the specific spinal subluxation caused by the curvature.

Imbalance: Sinus Infections

Manifestation: Inflammation of sinus cavities.
- Symptoms: Pain and pressure in sinus cavities, limitation of nasal inhalation, inflamed and stuffy upper respiratory region. Drainage of post nasal drip irritating throat.

Reiki Treatment: Full body.
- Facial area over, below, and beside eyes. Throat, colon, digestive tract and adrenals will be imbalanced. Use the pressure points on eye brow line of eye and below eye.

Nutritional Needs:
- Foods: Eliminate all mucus foods (see Respiratory Illnesses). Increase juices and water, fruits and vegetables. Limit grains and no wheat products unless sprouted.
- Herbs: Cayenne, aloe vera, rose hips, saw palmetto, mullein, garlic. Tea tree oil applied with cotton swab to inside of nose.
- Vitamins: B-complex, B6, C, A.
- Minerals: Zinc.
- Special Nutritional/Herbal Combinations: Sinus Blend, Colon Cleanse Combination, Build Combination, Fenugreek & Thyme, Colloidal Silver, Lung Expectorant Combination, Allergy & Lung Combination. Sinus Homeopathic Remedy.

- Homeopathic Tissue Salts: Calc. Sulp.

Environmental changes needed: Food and flora sensitivities; allergens; pollution.

Probable Esoteric Psychological Relationship: Tears held within from feeling that your will power is being directed by another's desires (giving up your power with resentment). Blockage of clear vision in personal matters due to responding to compelling force and pressure of a loved one or authority figure. Drainage of sinus—shedding of tears within; a need to express one's emotions and release through crying.

Chakra Center: Third, fifth, sixth.

Imbalance: Spinal Disorders

Manifestation: There are numerous disorders of the spine which need professional chiropractic care in conjunction with Reiki. What one must realize is that all disorders of our body affect the spine through the direct contact by the nerves from the spine to specific body part. Therefore, chiropractic medicine is an applicable adjunct modality with Reiki Plus.

Reiki Treatment: (See Scoliosis)

- *Psycho-Therapeutic Reiki Plus* and *SAT* to release emotional trauma held in the tissue and nerves.
- Spinal polarity running Reiki energy (see *Reiki Plus Natural Healing,* Chapter 7) treatments are to be done immediately following a Chiropractic adjustment to stabilize the muscles and tendons. Reiki will increase the rate of healing, eliminate the pain (occurring 3-4 hrs after an adjustment) and balance the body for any existing dysfunction.
- Teach the client the Cosmic Fire visualization technique, and advise them to do it three times daily for pain.

Nutritional Needs:

- Vitamins: Multiple, C.
- Herbs: Irish moss.
- Minerals: Manganese, chromium and zinc. Calcium Magnesium blend.
- Special Nutritional/Herbal Combinations: Joint & Structural Combination, MSM Combination Cream, Chinese Bone Support, Herbal Back Adjustment Blend.

Medical Referral: DNFT Chiropractic (does not create muscular trauma, as these techniques are gentle).

Probable Esoteric Psychological Relationship: Disproportionate distribution of one's stress and life's load; not being able to let go of and/or delegate responsibility.

Imbalance: Stomach Disorders

Manifestation: Inability to process foods, improper food combinations.

- Symptoms: Pain, indigestion.

Reiki Treatment:

- Full body; stomach, pancreas and liver-gallbladder.

Nutritional Needs:

- Foods: Elimination of incompatible foods, fruits, and vegetables. Too much fluid and alcohol with meal, heavy protein after salads or bread.
- Herbs: papaya, cayenne, peppermint oil.
- Vitamins: Betaine HCL may be needed to stimulate hydrochloric acid production in stomach; digestive enzymes for bile and pancreas may also be needed. Enzymes and HCL stimulants are needed on a regular basis in some individuals.
- Minerals: Magnesium.
- Special Nutritional/Herbal Combinations: Papaya Enzyme Blend, Enzyme Support Combination, Stomach Formula, Food Enzymes, Protein Digestion Combination, Chinese Digestive Support Blend, Digestive Support Blend. Intestinal Repair Combination and HP Herbal Fighter Combination if ulcer.
- Homeopathic Tissue Salts: Ferrum Phos. (gastritis), Kali Mur. (constipation), Natr. Phos. (acid stomach), Natr. Mur. (indigestion), Calc. Phos. (indigestion), Calc. Phos. (indigestion), Kali Phos. (indigestion from nerves), Mag. Phos. (hiccups and indigestion), Natr. Sulp.

Medical Referral: Nutritionist; Internist.

Environmental changes needed: Eating while under stress will contribute to digestive disorders, meditation extremely beneficial before mealtime to prepare body and mind.

Probable Esoteric Psychological Relationship: Security center - one's inability to digest foods can be a complex puzzle; however, we most often find that improper and overeating oftentimes occur as a sedation of insecurity and inability (or desire) to communicate.

Chakra Center: Third, fifth.

Imbalance: Stroke

Manifestation: Calcium deficiency on organic level in the muscle, tissue and bone structure, resulting in a weakness and/or inability to use the organ involved; often from previous febrile conditions weakening the organ.

- Symptoms: Severe seizure or attack often termed apoplexy.

Reiki Treatment:
- Full body; all areas of head, face, and neck, #3 alternate for proper blood flow. Treat as soon after a stroke as possible. Continued daily treatments for sustained improvement to occur. Treat parts of body affected.
- *Psycho-Therapeutic Reiki Plus* for understanding the emotions underlying the chronic disorder.
- *PSEB* to align the associated Chakra bodies

Nutritional Needs:
- Foods: Green leafy vegetables, nuts (unsalted and raw). Eliminate sugar and refined foods. Protein from fish and poultry (organically raised). Omega 3 Fatty acids.
- Herbs: Cayenne, burdock root and seed, chaparral, garlic, ginger bath and tea. Butcher's Broom to inhibit abnormal blood clotting.
- Vitamins: A & C prevent strokes. A, C, B-complex, granulated lecithin, E (low dosage, 100 I.U's increased weekly to 800 daily).
- Minerals: Calcium and magnesium.
- Special Nutritional/Herbal Combinations: After stroke give Suma Formula with B6. Circulatory Combination, Grape Seed Pine Bark Combination, Gingko & Hawthorne Combination.
- Homeopathic Tissue Salts: Calc. and Mag. Phos.

Medical Referral: Medical attention immediately.

Environmental changes needed: Identification of personal reaction to environmental stress.

Probable Esoteric Psychological Relationship: An uncontrolled release of internal stress resulting most often in paralysis of a part (or parts) of the body's mental and physical capacity. Origin of causal factor and resultant body part provides insight of esoteric psychological relationships between body and mind.

Chakra Center: First, fourth and sixth.

Imbalance: Thyroid Imbalances

Manifestation: Hyper (over active) or hypo (under active) thyroid function. Hyperthyroidism: increased metabolism, goiters, and disturbances of the autonomic nervous system mark this Imbalance. Hypothyroidism: decreased metabolic rate, tiredness and lethargy to include body temperature control mark this disorder.

Reiki Treatment:
- Full body; throat and adrenals.
- *Psycho-Therapeutic Reiki Plus* for understanding the emotions underlying the chronic disorder.
- *PSEB* to align the associated Chakra bodies

Nutritional Needs:

- Foods: Iodine foods (onions and seafood's). "Excessive" cabbage inhibits utilization of iodine in thyroid gland. Therefore, prolonged use of Reiki Slaw could result in energy loss. Supplement diet with Kelp to provide natural source of iodine.
- Herbs: Kelp. Hawthorne if irregular heartbeat with hyperthyroidism.
- Vitamins: C and E (Vit. E is considered harmful in hyperthyroidism). Excess B1 affects thyroid and insulin production.
- Minerals: Calcium and magnesium may be needed. Cobalt should be avoided, thyroid enlargement has resulted from overexposure.
- Special Nutritional/Herbal Combinations:

Hyperthyroidism – Thyroid Combination #1, CoQ10, magnesium, Stress Formula, Chinese Stress Combination. Hypothyroidism – Thyroid Combination #2 or Thyroid Combination #3, Black currant or evening primrose oil, potassium. Glandular System Blend. Homeopathic Tissue Salts: Silica, Calc. Phos., Natr. Phos. (goiter), Calc. Sulp.

Medical Referral: Internist; Endocrinologist; Nutritionist.

Environmental changes needed: Examination of working area may be necessary.

Probable Esoteric Psychological Relationship: On one level, most thyroid Imbalances are correspondent to the degree that one's repression or expression of inner feelings are, or are not handled.

Body Parts: Throat - adrenals.

Chakra Center: Third, fifth.

Imbalance: Throat, Ulcerated, Sore, or Congested

- Symptoms: Pain, rawness and congestion with mucus from post nasal drip.

Reiki Treatment:

- Full body; head and throat.
- *Psycho-Therapeutic Reiki Plus* for understanding the emotions underlying the disorder.

Nutritional Needs: (See Inflammation, Fever).

- Foods: Eliminate mucus foods, sugar and refined foods. Add juices of vegetables and apple.
- Herbs: Cayenne, sassafras (inflamed); sage and oak (ulcerated); red raspberry and slippery elm, licorice, mullein and/or bayberry (sore throat), garlic.
- Vitamins: B-complex, Vit. C (1,000 mg, 3 or more times daily), A, E, D, B5, B6.
- Minerals: Zinc, magnesium.

- Special Nutritional/Herbal Combinations: May need bowel cleansing if from post nasal drip: use Colon Cleanse Combination & Sinus Blend, along with Fenugreek and Thyme to dry excess mucous.
- Homeopathic Tissue Salts: Mag. Phos., Silica (ulcers), Natr. Phos. (sore with creamy coating), Calc. Phos. (swallowing pain).

Probable Esoteric Psychological Relationship: Identification to whom one wishes to communicate deep inner emotional feelings and why suppression is being held within.

Body Parts: Coccyx, adrenals, thyroid.

Chakra Center: First, third, fifth.

Imbalance: Tumors

Manifestation: An abnormal growth of cells parasitic in nature, a rising from a host cell, however, independent and progressive in their growth. Malignant or non malignant, growing at various rates and in any part of the body. An inability to filter unhealthy tissue cells from body.

- Symptoms: A swelling, hard or soft in texture.

Reiki Treatment:

- Full body; tumor host organs and chakras, pancreas, thymus, first and second chakra, spleen and pituitary. Throat center will also be blocked. Lymphatic system (arms and legs).
- *Psycho-Therapeutic Reiki Plus* for understanding the emotions underlying the disorder.
- *PSEB* to align the associated Chakra bodies
- Fasting on vegetable or apple juice for three days, with proper fasting procedures.

Nutritional Needs: (See Fibroid Cyst).

- Foods: Eliminate caffeine, fatty foods, skins from chicken and polysaturated and hydrogenated oils. Add Kelp and red cabbage.
- Herbs: yellow dock, burdock root, black walnut, Pau D'Arco.
- Vitamins: B-complex, B6. Reduce Vit. E, PABA and Folic Acid. Lecithin, CoQ10.
- Minerals: Zinc, germanium, selenium, manganese; multiple.
- Special Nutritional/Herbal Combinations: Essiac Tea, Detoxification Blend, Food Enzymes, Enzyme Support Combination, Special Formula #1, Pau D'Arco Program, Red Clover Combination, Liver Support Combination #2, Antioxidant Combination. Fatty Tumor: Lipase Enzyme, Chickweed, Butcher's Broom, Immune Blend.
- Homeopathic Tissue Salts: Kali Mur., Calc. Fluor. (breasts), Silica (when suppurating).

Medical Referral: Have blood chemistry analyzed and read by trained physician-nutritionist.

Probable Esoteric Psychological Relationship: A mass of thought-forms collected and invading a part of the body as an out growth of one's specific Imbalance of emotions. The system of the body and/or the organ or tissue area where the tumor is found will help clarify the emotional and chakra origin needed to be understood by the individual.

Chakra Center: First, second, fourth, sixth, seventh and eighth.

Imbalance: Ulcers

Manifestation: A large accumulation of dead cells that have decayed and formed pus, residing on a lining of tissue; i.e., stomach, leg, intestines, vagina.

- Symptoms: Pain and sensitivity localized to ulceration.

Reiki Treatment:

- Full body; specific area ulcerated; pancreas, stomach, gallbladder if within digestive system.
- *Psycho-Therapeutic Reiki Plus* for understanding the deeply held patterns of emotions underlying the chronic disorder.
- *PSEB* to align the associated chakra bodies

Nutritional Needs:

- Foods: Eliminate mucus foods, sugars, refined foods, caffeine and alcohol, cola and unnecessary stimulants; add raw cabbage and it juice.
- Herbs: Cayenne, comfrey root, aloe vera, alfalfa, papaya.
- Vitamins: U, alfalfa, B-complex, A, E.
- Minerals: Multiple.
- Special Nutritional/Herbal Combinations: Diabetic ulcers- clean the bowels with Colon Cleanse Combination; apply tea tree oil, golden salve or healing ac cream. Vitamins A, C and Bioflavonoids important. Bone Combination made in to a poultice and applied to ulcerated areas. Duodenal/Stomach ulcers: HP Herbal Fighter Combination, Intestinal Repair Combination, Bone Combination to heal ulceration, Ulcer Combination. Eliminate Stress: Stress Formula, Stress Combination. Support Pancreas to do their job to produce alkaline enzymes to neutralize acidic stomach enzymes with Pancreas Formula #2; Stomach Formula to neutralize excess acid in stomach. Kava kava will soothe pain, and golden seal or capsicum will stop bleeding.
- Homeopathic Tissue Salts: Kali Mur (white fibrous discharge); Ferrum Phos. (febrile conditions); Silica (extremities, fistulous ulcers, hard, swollen glands); Calc. Fluor (bone area).

Medical Referral: Internist, Gastroenterologist, Nutritionist.

Probable Esoteric Psychological Relationship: Emotionally being eaten away by holding in anger and unpleasant thought-forms. Understanding where stress is being allowed to disrupt one's flow of harmony.

Chakra Centers: Third, fifth.

Imbalance: Vaginitis (See Yeast Infections)

Manifestation: Inflammation of the vagina.

- Symptoms: Irritation, burning, itching of vagina oftentimes with mucus discharge.

Reiki Treatment:

- Full body; over opening of vagina with other hand placed over public region covering uterus, ovaries and vagina. Hand between the legs should not contact the clothing of client.

Nutritional Needs: (See Infections, Inflammations.)

- Foods: Eliminate processed foods, yeast and sugars, caffeine's and chemicals. Add: Protein and green leafy vegetables. Consider Candida diet.
- Herbs: Slippery elm, motherwort, garlic. Pau D'Arco tea.
- Vitamins: E, A, D, C, B-complex.
- Minerals: Multiple, zinc, selenium, manganese.
- Special Nutritional/Herbal Combinations: Intestinal Flora Blend, Candida Fighter.
- Homeopathic Tissue Salts: Ferrum Phos.

Medical Referral: OB/GYN.

Environmental changes needed: Feminine hygiene may need improving. Loose fitting clothing.

Probable Esoteric Psychological Relationship: May relate to desire to prevent or limit sexual contact with mate, and/or childhood traumas. For further insight, refer to book by Christiane Northrup, MD *Women's Bodies, Women's Wisdom.*

Chakra Center: Second, fourth

Imbalance: Varicose Veins

Manifestation: Distention of the walls of the vein, a brittle condition subject to rupturing.

- Symptoms: Ruptured blood veins under surface of skin, swelling. Pain to stand in extreme conditions. Can affect major veins, as well as smaller veins of body.

Reiki Treatment:

- Full body; see specific diagram—place one hand on #4 front and other hand in groin over femoral vein until feet are warmed, then treat any ruptures. Treat both legs.
- *Psycho-Therapeutic Reiki Plus* for understanding the emotions underlying the chronic disorder.
- *PSEB* to align the associated chakra bodies

- Exercise in the form of walking, swimming and bicycling. Excessive sitting is considered to aggravate and lead to varicose veins.

Nutritional Needs:
- Foods: Seeds, nuts, grains, buckwheat, millet, raw vegetables and fruit. Juices of fruit, especially carrot, rose hips, black currants and citrus, for Vit. C and bioflavonoids.
- Herbs: Butcher's Broom, white oak bark, cayenne, aloe vera, kelp, hawthorne, garlic.
- Vitamins: B-complex, B6, C, (throughout day).
- Minerals: Calcium, magnesium, multiple.
- Special Nutritional/Herbal Combinations: Varicose Veins Blend, Gingko & Hawthorne, Grape Seed Pine Bark Combination, Chlorophyll, Heart Support Formula.
- Homeopathic Tissue Salts: Calc. Fluor., Ferrum Phos.

Medical Referral: Physician, Nutritionist, Naturopath.

Probable Esoteric Psychological Relationship: When the personality of the individual has become restrictive and brittle, hardening of the connective tissue (veins, gums, etc.) takes place. Letting go of possessiveness and rigid control is crucial to reverse the attitude.

Body Parts: Connective tissue.

Chakra Center: Third.

Imbalance: Weight Control

Manifestation: Improper assimilation of foods and the storage of food as fat in the body. Blockage or restriction of thyroid and pituitary glands to regulate stress and normal metabolism.

Reiki Treatment:
- Full body; head, throat, adrenals, liver, pancreas, gallbladder, and reproductive chakra. Combining yoga and breath exercises, especially shoulder stands to activate the thyroid.
- *SAT* if spinal conflict involved.
- *Psycho-Therapeutic Reiki Plus* for understanding the emotions underlying the chronic disorder.
- *PSEB* to align the associated chakra bodies
- Fad diets can be dangerous. An important factor is not starving yourself, it does not work. Eating small, properly balanced meals, more frequently is best for weight reduction. Waiting too long between meals affects the fat storage process in the body, because the body knows it is being starved and changes food more rapidly to fat to fuel the body when unfed.

Nutritional Needs:
- Foods: Reiki Slaw during fast for 3-5 days to cleanse the system. Decrease excessive carbohydrates, fats, fatty proteins, fried foods.

Increase raw vegetables and limit fruits (sugar). Linoleic acid, an unsaturated fat, is needed in a 2 to 1 ratio to burn saturated fats. Heating saturated fats destroys properties.

- Herbs: kelp, chickweed, bladderwack
- Vitamins: F (linoleic acid, 12 tsp. sunflower seeds or 18 pecan halves provide daily need), E. Amino acids, L-Arginine, L-Onetime, and L-Lysine in proper ratio have been found essential in production of HGH from the pituitary gland to control weight.
- Minerals: Iodine—If you are an "excessive" cabbage consumer, you are decreasing its utilization in your diet. In which case, Kelp is needed to offset this effect.

Special Nutritional/Herbal Combinations:
To Gain Weight: Saw Palmetto, alfalfa, chamomile. Alfalfa Combination, Spiraling Combination, Food Enzymes, B-Complex, Protein Combination, Gland Support Combination, Amino Acid Combination. If thyroid overactive: Thyroid Combination #1. Consider parasites to be a factor: Chinese Parasite Cleanse, Parasite Homeopathic Remedy.
To Lose Weight: Cleansing the colon is important: Colon Cleanse Combination, Intestinal Cleanse. To burn fat and feel full: Thermo genesis Formula #1 with Ephedra, Thermo genesis Formula #2 with Synephrine, Collagen Formula, Garcinia Combination, Remove Fat Combination, Food Enzymes, Cellulite Formula, Pyruvate, Chickweed Combination, Meal Replacement, Gymnema Combination. Homeopathic Remedies: Appetite Control, Calor.

Medical Referral: Nutritionist.

Probable Esoteric Psychological Relationship: So often metabolism is restricted, leading to weight imbalance from closure at the emotional communication level. Food supplements the non-communication. Closure blocks the thyroid function. Security, communication and self worth are needed. Not feeling loved or needed. Creative expression essential for providing a person the feeling of being worthy of love. Individual normally is holding anger inside the heart.

Chakra Center: All Centers could be participating, third, fourth and fifth are probably going to be strongly affected.

Imbalance: Whiplash

Manifestation: Normally caused by impact thrusting cervical vertebra backwards with the head. Often associated with rear-end collisions in automobile accidents.

- Symptoms: Discomfort and immobility of the neck.

Reiki Treatment:

- Full body; treat entire spinal column.

- *SAT* for understanding the deeply held patterns of emotions underlying the disorder.

Nutritional Needs:
- Foods: Green leafy vegetables.
- Herbs: Valerian (pain), Irish moss (calcium).
- Vitamins: B-complex.
- Minerals: Chromium, zinc.
- Special Nutritional/Herbal Combinations: Joint & Structural Combination, Chinese Inflammation Combination, Natural Pain Relief Combination, MSM Combination Cream, Chinese Bone Support, Bone Combination, Skeletal Builder, Herbal Back Adjustment Blend.
- Homeopathic Tissue Salts: Kali Phos. Mag. Phos, Calc. Phos.

Medical Referral: Chiropractic examinations and treatment, massage and/or physical therapy.

Imbalance: Yeast Infections (Candida Albicans)

Manifestation: Infection by yeast grown fungi in the body. Most commonly associated with vaginal tract. However, fungi have invaded other body parts.
- Symptoms: Itching and mucus discharge from vagina. This disease is commonly called the "missing diagnosis" and is related to many physical, emotional, and mental disorders.

Reiki Treatment:
- Full body; treat same as vaginitis.
- *Psycho-Therapeutic Reiki Plus* for understanding the emotions underlying the chronic disorder.
- *PSEB* to align the associated chakra bodies

Nutritional Needs:
- Foods: Eliminate sugars, refined foods, caffeine, and other allergens, mucus foods, alcohol, and drugs. Acid foods, if not allergic to them, help offset breeding ground for yeast.
- Herbs: Pau D'Arco, garlic, tea tree oil, una de gato, bayberry, plantain, red raspberry
- Vitamins: Multiple. Acidophilus capsules, caprylic acid.
- Minerals: Multiple.
- Special Nutritional/Herbal Combinations: Candida Fighter, Candida Homeopathic, Food Enzymes, Intestinal Flora Blend, Chinese Parasite Cleanse.
- For Nails and Toes: Soak in Pau d' Arco and tea tree oil 15 minutes per day, or use grapefruit seed extract mixed in water.
- For Vaginal: douche with one half cup Pau D'Arco tea and five drops grapefruit seed extract, or with garlic and Intestinal Flora Blend in one half cup Pau D'Arco tea.

Medical Referral: Medical nutritionist, Allergist who is a physician or works concurrently with a physician. Requires special diets and medication.

Environmental changes needed: Allergy foods and stress must be identified.

Probable Esoteric Psychological Relationship: Any number of emotional relationships that come from blocking the creative flow of life energy.

Pages for Notes

Reiki Comes of Age

by John E. Steele, Sacred Path Reiki Master

Just eight short years ago, I received an attunement into the ancient spiritual healing modality known as Reiki. It was a time when we still believed Reiki was lost in Japan after World War II and that Mikao Usui was a Christian minister. It was a time when Reiki was still a mysterious art. It was a time when no regulation of Reiki existed in our country, a time when we were all taught that being a minister in a church was enough to legally practice Reiki. My, how fast things change these days.

We now know that Reiki is alive and well in Japan, that Mikao Usui was a Buddhist monk. There are books which strip Reiki bare, revealing all its secrets, killing the mystery, for better or worse and hit the best seller list as a result. It's a time when individuals attempt trademarks, attempt monopolistic legislation, a time when boards of massage therapy usurp authority over Reiki under the guise of public protection.

And in the process, decisions are made that define Reiki on the national level, without the direct involvement of those within the Reiki community. At the time of this writing, there are three states[1] whose boards of massage therapy have somehow come to the conclusion that Reiki constitutes massage and therefore require all Reiki practitioners and Masters to be certified massage therapists. There are seven states[2] with pending legislation to form boards of massage therapy which could, potentially, arrive at the conclusion and require masters and practitioners to be certified massage therapists.

In 1998, after years of claiming that Reiki constituted massage, the New York board of massage therapy was pressured by a united Reiki community into holding their *first* formal hearing to determine whether or not Reiki constituted massage! Early the next year, the hard fought battle resulted in a victory: the board formally voted and admitted that Reiki was not massage.

Texas saw a different attempt to control Reiki in 1999: legislation was introduced into the state legislature that would grant two schools of Reiki the exclusive right to teach and practice in that state. The Texans for Reiki and Fairness group formed. After a highly effective letter writing campaign and a "Reiki Day" inside the Texan capital building as well as other great efforts, the legislature was well enough informed (and relaxed enough from the free Reiki treatments), to permanently kill the bill. This same year saw an attempt to obtain a U.S. trademark for the word "Reiki" by a nationally known school. Great efforts resulted in this attempt making a peaceful transition a few months later.

In front of us at the time of this writing are 11 great opportunities as Reiki comes of age. The first three are to reverse the opinions of the boards of massage in the states that currently claim Reiki constitutes massage. The next seven are to get involved in the pending legislation in the states that are working to form massage boards to prevent further regulation of Reiki by these outsiders.

The last Great Opportunity as Reiki comes of age is for all involved in Reiki to set about the difficult and demanding task of defining Reiki on the national level as a spiritual hands on healing modality, constitutionally separated from the state. If we do

---

[1] North Dakota, Florida, and Utah.

[2] Illinois, Michigan, Minnesota, Massachusetts, North Carolina, Georgia and Montana

not participate in the definition of Reiki at the national level, it will continue to be defined by others at the state level. If we do not actively participate in the national definition of Reiki, we will continue to spend our time and energy defining what Reiki is not, working at the state level. If a Master looks to the west and says "It doesn't affect my school." What will happen when another Master looks east and says the same?

If indeed Reiki is a spiritual hands on healing modality, which I believe it is, then I say it is time for the nationally recognized Reiki schools, branches, organizations, Masters, authors and activists to come together in a cooperative council with a three-fold purpose: to establish a set of professional standards all can agree upon, to establish a minimum set of requirements that all can agree upon and to form a federally recognized church in which those of us who have given ourselves over to this sacred task can be ordained, forever free to practice this wonderment called "Reiki". This church would be created as a service to those practicing Reiki. None would be compelled to join. It would be available and optional. Schools would have the option to become satellite churches. Individual Masters and practitioners could become ordained, regardless of lineage, of religion, as long as they meet the minimum standards and agree to the professional ethics. The formal of this church will define Reiki nationally, forever ending massage board interference, as well as legislative attempts.

If we do not seek the spiritual solution to meet our needs, others will find solutions that meet their needs. If we do not seek to define ourselves, to regulate ourselves, then we indeed, by default, leave that to those who have other motives, other concerns, other intentions. If those of us who are involved in Reiki do not believe that minimum standards are to the benefit of Reiki, I assure you that there are others outside of Reiki who do. If we who are involved in Reiki do not believe that a code of professional standards is desirable, I assure you that there are others outside of Reiki that do. If we do not do these things, or similar things, for ourselves, there are plenty of others who will and are doing these things for us, not with us.

It's time for the greater Reiki community to realize that all of our lineages begin with Mikao Usui and that it continues with the next seven generations of Masters and Practitioners. It is time for the greater Reiki community to become the United Reiki Community as Reiki comes of age.

Namaste,
Rev. John E. Steele
Sacred Path Reiki Master
May 10th, 2000

Intuitive Evaluation of Client Consciousness

Learn how the Masters of the Brotherhood of Light have been directing your spiritual journey since the day you said, "There has to be another way."

This course combines the steps and stages of guidance and growth directed by the Masters of each Ray of Spiritual Consciousness and aligns it with your Soul's journey through the lessons of the Personality. A powerful class that contains essential material for spiritual healing and recognizing your potential for infusing your soul in the Christ Consciousness of Light. Learn what the colors surrounding you or your clients and friends really mean. Know what Ray you or they are evolving through and when the Rays of the Personality will be completed and the infusions of the soul's permanent Rays will take place.

6 - 90" Tapes $100.00 Review Tapes $50.00

Astro-Physiology and Anatomy

Your will learn an applied method of Spiritual Astrology developed over the past quarter of a century by David's daily use of astrology to understand the unique and divine nature of the soul, not only for understanding but as an invaluable aid in healing. **50 Credit Hours.**

Segment 1: An astrological foundation is built to develop a spiritual and transpersonal perspective to astrology. Natal information, Chakras, Aspects, signs and houses are studied.
7- 90" Tapes $90.00 (includes Chakra Astrology by David G. Jarrell.)

Segment 2: Learn recognition of physical, emotional and psychological disorders, knowledge of the planetary dominion of each chakra and its associated anatomy to the CNS, and understand how to read the potential of spinal imbalances by natal aspects. Interpret natal charts spiritually.
7- 90" Tapes $75.00

Segment 3: Learn Aspect delineation of Natal, Transit s and Progressions and how the cycles of the planets direct our growth. Gain an understanding of the Spiritual transpersonal Ego compared to the Personality's ego.
7- 90" Tapes $75.00

Applied Esoteric Psychology and Anatomy

Esoteric Psychology teaches the practitioner of Natural Healing the keys to listening and hearing what your client is really asking you to hear. The student will learn procedures to assess the client for obtaining the thesis of the client's psycho- physical challenge. Techniques to develop insight to see the subtle implications presented by the client's words that describe the conditions (symptoms). The proper listening to the client's words and description of conditions will provide delineation and synthesis. The reward of this technique is learning how to redirect the psycho- physical towards wellness—the ability to handle difficult situations without debilitating stress.

Objectives: The student will learn the objectives and techniques of the Client's Interview:

1. Proper listening techniques.
2. Assessment of symptomatic information.
3. Psycho-physical profile.
4. Redirection of mind-body-emotions towards wellness.
5. Selecting the proper healing modality for the client's needs.

6 - 90" Tapes $100.00 plus book *Review Tapes: $50.00

Esoteric Anatomy and Psychology by David G. Jarrell $25.00. Book only $10.00 if both Tape Sets are purchased.

Esoteric Anatomy teaches the Practitioner the fundamental tools of Esoteric Anatomy and Psychology. The technique is for integrating subjective symptoms through intuitive observation by the Practitioner. Esoteric Anatomy - understanding how the Personality vs. the Spiritual consciousness must be approached to properly interpret a client's process of challenge.

Objectives:

1. Esoteric Anatomy: Learn to delineate the body's psycho-physical, psycho-emotional and psycho-mental dynamics.
2. Chakra Anatomy: Learn the relationship of the Etheric Bodies' and the neurological connection to the glands and organs by chakra dominion.
3. Learn an integrative approach to unite your working knowledge of Esoteric and Chakra Anatomy.
4. Learn the function of Faith, Trust and Forgiveness.

6 - 90" Tapes $100.00 Review Tapes: $50.00

Breath of Light℠

An Illuminating experience - In two hours you will learn: How *Light* enters the body and charges it with vital energy; How *Light* flows to the organs, glands and tissue; How your emotions unconsciously limit your receptivity of the *Light*; How to Master your emotional responses to old negative patterns; How to take charge of your physical, emotional and spiritual health; How to use energy exercises that direct *Light* to strengthen the body and reduce or even eliminate pain. Experience David Jarrell's beautiful and healing **Forgiveness Meditation**

3 Credit Hours 2 -60" Tapes $20.00

The Term "Review Price" applies to a student of Reiki Plus® who is a graduate of the Seminar and wishes to purchase the same class tapes for continued study.

Meditation Tapes

Expand the depth of your Healings with David's beautifully inspired Meditations

The Forgiveness Meditation

This meditation leads you through the five steps of forgiveness for any challenge you are ready to resolve in your life; a powerful and moving healing experience.

The Fairy Tale Meditation

A regression meditation used in our **Reiki Plus®** First Degree classes, this tape will help you to understand your free-will soul choices in this lifetime and the life themes you have chosen to work with.

Side 2 has the **Invocation of the Masters Ceremony** (Candle lighting ritual channeling the Masters).

The Transmutation Meditation

A guided meditation designed to help you transmute any issue you are working with in your life; meet your spirit teacher and gain spiritual insight on this wondrous journey through your Etheric Bodies.

All three for $25.00 Or $10.00 each

Reiki Plus Professional Practitioner's Certification

The Professional Practitioner's Certification can be completed in your own home, except for the **Third Degree Practitioner** training. Our tutorial **Knowledge Reviews** guide your study through the Tapes and Books, providing a comprehensive and thorough education. For the beginner you receive your **Initiations** through spiritual transmissions while you meditate, directly from David and Richelle Jarrell. A crossover student from any other system of Reiki may elect to pay for Reiki Plus® initiations along with their tape purchase(s).

The Professional Practitioner's Certification Program consist of Reiki Plus First, Second, Second Degree Psycho-Therapeutic Reiki Plus® and Third Degree training and Initiations.

I. Reiki Plus® First Degree

This seminar is designed to teach techniques to use with the self and with clients to promote healing, relaxation and the reduction of stress. Learn how to activate, direct and apply Reiki healing to self and others to give a total body Reiki treatment; appreciate the human energy system with its natural restorative and balancing mechanisms; understand how Reiki is an independent healing system, as well as an adjunct to all healing processes; identify hand positions to be used with selected disorders and diseases; understand that Reiki is a self-growth tool facilitating personal wellness of mind, body & emotions.

a. Reiki Plus® Tapes w/o Initiation: $100.00

b. Reiki Plus® Tapes with Initiation: $200.00

Reiki Plus® Natural Healing by David G. Jarrell
included for $20.00 with Taped Class.

II. Second Degree Reiki Plus®

Prerequisite: Second Degree Reiki. Please send a photocopy of your Second Degree Certificate. Learn the mystical aspects of Second Degree; the activation of Second Degree Energy; Distant Healing techniques; heightened intuitive sensitivity. The material is tied together with information on the Eight Etheric Bodies, and Esoteric Anatomy and Psychology.

a. Reiki Plus® Tapes w/o Initiation: $100.00

b. Reiki Plus® Tapes with Initiation: $300.00

Reiki Plus® Professional Practitioner's Manual for Second Degree, 3rd Edition by David and Richelle Jarrell **included for $20.00 with Taped Class.**

III. Second Degree Psycho-Therapeutic Reiki Plus®

Identify psycho-physical, emotional and mental imbalances and know when **Psycho-Therapeutic Reiki Plus®** is an appropriate modality. Learn several approaches to opening the client to accepting God's Forgiveness and Divine Love – the essential element necessary for a complete and irreversible healing. Learn several approaches of the **Psycho-Therapeutic Reiki Plus® Technique.**

Students of Second Degree Initiation wishing to take this class, please submit a photocopy of your Second Degree Certificate with your Order. Credit Hours and Certification of Completion of Advanced Second Degree is awarded after completion of the Practicum and submission of the healing Treatment Forms.

All Students of Home Study Program: Tapes and Book: $300.00

IV. Third Degree Practitioner's Training and Initiation.

This final class of the Practitioner's Program is completed with direct training with your Reiki Plus Teacher. During the two or three days you will receive the two Initiations we give for this level of healing energy. You will learn how to integrate all of the education you have learned from your initial three classes into a synthesis for understanding and application.

Reiki Plus Third Degree 2 – 3 day Seminar is $500.00.

Order Form

Visa/MC accepted. Please send check or money order to the address below. Orders may be Faxed or Emailed. Please add $3.00 for s/h. Orders over $50.00 postage free within the USA.

Name____

Address____

City_____________________________State______Zip_________

PH_____________________Email________________________

Credit Card (Visa/MC)_____________________________________

Expiration Date_______________

Signature____

Total Charge $_______________

I would like to order the following tapes:_______________________

____

____

____

Receive a 20% Discount

on your first Order - unlimited choice of classes

Visit us online at www.reikiplus.com

Mail your Order to:

Reiki Plus
David and Richelle Jarrell
707 Barcelona Rd
Key Largo, FL 33037

Call us at (305) 451-9881
Fax your order to (305) 451-9841

Order Form